Achieving Financial Freedom: A Comprehensive Guide

Foreward

In an era defined by rapid technological advancements like NextGen AI and unprecedented global connectivity, Gen Z stands at the forefront of a new financial frontier. The landscape of financial management has evolved dramatically, offering both extraordinary opportunities and unique challenges. This book, Achieving Financial Freedom: A Comprehensive Collection, is designed with the intent to guide Gen Z through the intricate techniques of modern finance, providing a 360-degree coverage of all essential aspects to help readers to not only plan but also execute through real life experiences.

As digital natives, you as readers have unparalleled access to information and tools in a comprehensive way. Yet, the sheer volume of choices can be overwhelming. From the allure of cryptocurrencies to the complexities of gig economy earnings, the paths to financial freedom are diverse and multifaceted. This guide aims to demystify these paths, equipping you with the knowledge and strategies needed to navigate the financial world with confidence and foresight.

The author delves into the foundational principles of budgeting, saving, and investing, while also exploring innovative approaches like leveraging technology for passive income and mastering the nuances of the digital market. The goal is to provide a holistic understanding that goes beyond mere financial literacy, fostering a mindset that embraces adaptability, resilience, and strategic thinking.

Financial freedom is not a one-size-fits-all concept and perhaps cannot be enlightened by a few seconds of 'reels', 'shorts' and those meant to attract followers and likes. It is deeply personal, shaped by individual aspirations, values, and circumstances. This book encourages you to define what financial freedom means to you, helping you set SMART goals and align your financial journey with your core values. Whether you dream of early retirement, entrepreneurial success, or simply the peace of mind that comes from financial stability, the insights and techniques shared here will serve as your roadmap.

Embark on this journey with an open mind and a determined spirit. The future of finance is yours to shape, and with the right tools and knowledge, you can build a life of abundance, freedom, and fulfillment.

Welcome to your comprehensive guide on financial planning.
Murali Hara Gopal,
Chartered accountant,
UK & Europe Insurance Solutions Head,
HCLTech

I have known Rajesh and his lovely wife, Hema, for three decades now. We met at work, became acquaintances, and drifted apart for almost two decades. Social media connected us back, our mutual interest in writing, cinema and politics rejuvenated our friendship. Rajesh, A successful IT professional, a passionate photographer and a writer, both fiction and non-fiction. Clarity is the key ingredient in his work, both photography and writing. I am not a fiancé major endorsing this book, as an avid reader, I grasp the basic nuts and bolts of financial tips this text provides, a sincere effort, reflecting the author's journey in financial planning. Rajesh has mirrored the work of an architect in presenting the building blocks of financial freedom. Like any first stage of a beautiful building, starting with foundation of finance, raising the walls of Income, sheltering your walls of income with a roof of investment, to achieve self-sufficiency, sustenance, and abundance. A bonus package on budgeting with frugal mind set, wrapped with a new idea, 'fire Movement' a series of 'out of box' ideas, with the intent to keep your monies 'inside your box'. A compelling financial guide, a sensible addition to your personal library collection, and a must read for financial awakening.

Jayashree Venkataramani
Alberta,
Canada

Preface

Investing labyrinths: Where countless paths lead to a single goal

Remember stepping into the world of investing decades ago? It felt like navigating a labyrinth, with whispers of "hot stocks" and "surefire bets" echoing through the halls. Back then, guidance was scarce, and the path to financial wisdom paved with costly missteps. (Who among us has not emerged a bit lighter in the wallet after a foray into the wrong investment?)

Fast forward to today's information age. Social media bombards us with a constant stream of investment options. It's a double-edged sword: a treasure trove of knowledge, but also enough details to leave you feeling overwhelmed and paralyzed by indecision.

The truth is there is no one-size-fits-all approach to building wealth. Investing, like trading or navigating the gig economy, is a deeply personal journey. Risk tolerance varies wildly, and what works wonders for your neighbor might leave you flat on your face.

The ever-evolving financial landscape throws curveballs our way, too. The rise of the gig economy and the enigmatic world of cryptocurrency add new twists and turns to the investment maze.

That is why I've embarked on this mission to create a comprehensive guide - a map, if you will, to illuminate the various paths within the investment labyrinth. This book won't tell you what to do, but rather, show you what *can* be done.

Think of it as a buffet of possibilities, where you can explore real estate ventures, delve into daily trading strategies, or consider the flexibility of the gig economy. Each chapter will introduce you to a different investment option, equipping you with the foundational knowledge to delve deeper and chart your own course to financial success.

So, whether you dream of becoming a real estate mogul, a master day trader, a thriving gig worker, or a real-estate mogul, this book is your springboard. Let's turn that labyrinth of options into a clear path towards achieving your financial goals.

Rajesh Srinivasan

What is in this book?

This guide is designed to be a roadmap for your journey towards financial freedom. Financial freedom can be defined differently for everyone, but refers to the state where your passive income (money earned without actively working) covers your living expenses. This allows you to choose how you spend your time, free from financial constraints.

The guide will be broken down into the following sections, each around 5-7 pages long, providing a comprehensive overview of various strategies:

Part 1: Building Your Financial Foundation

- **Understanding Financial Freedom:** This section will delve into the concept of financial freedom, explore different definitions, and help you identify what it means for you.
- **Assessing Your Current Situation:** Here, you'll learn how to analyze your income, expenses, debts, and assets. This financial snapshot will be crucial for creating your personalized plan.
- **Building a Budget and Tracking Expenses:** Discover how to create a workable budget that allocates your income towards essential needs, savings, and debt repayment. You'll also learn effective expense tracking methods.

Part 2: Increasing Your Income

- **Maximizing Your Current Income:** Explore strategies to increase your income within your current job, such as negotiating raises, taking on additional responsibilities, or acquiring new skills.
- **Developing Multiple Income Streams:** Learn about various ways to generate income outside your regular job. This could include freelance work, starting a side hustle, or investing in income-producing assets.

Part 3: Living Frugally and Saving Wisely

- **Adopting a Frugal Mindset:** This section explores the concept of mindful spending, focusing on needs over wants. You will learn strategies to reduce expenses in different areas of your life without sacrificing quality.
- **Debt Management:** Discover effective methods to tackle debt, including debt consolidation, snowball or avalanche methods, and strategies to avoid future debt accumulation.
- **Saving Strategies:** Learn about different savings vehicles such as high-yield savings accounts, retirement accounts (IRAs, 401(k)s), and emergency funds. You will also explore automatic savings techniques.

Part 4: Investing for Growth

- **Understanding Investments:** Get familiar with the different investment options available, including stocks, bonds, mutual funds, ETFs, and real estate.
- **Developing an Investment Strategy:** Learn about asset allocation, diversification, and risk tolerance. These factors will help you create a personalized investment portfolio aligned with your goals.
- **Building Long-Term Wealth:** Explore strategies for long-term wealth creation through compound interest and dollar-cost averaging investment approaches.
- **Unveiling the Crypto Market:** Understand the world of Cryptocurrency

Part 5: Building Passive Income Streams

- **Rental Properties:** Learn about the potential benefits and challenges of investing in rental properties for passive income generation.
- **Dividends and Interest:** Explore how to invest in assets that generate regular passive income through dividends (stocks) or interest (bonds).
- **Business Ownership:** This section discusses the possibility of building a business that can operate with minimal ongoing management, generating passive

income.

Part 6: Maintaining and Protecting Your Wealth

- **Tax Planning:** Learn strategies for tax-efficient investing and minimizing your tax burden to maximize your financial gains.
- **Risk Management:** Explore methods to protect your wealth from unforeseen circumstances like market downturns or emergencies.
- **Estate Planning:** Understand the importance of estate planning and create a will to ensure your assets are distributed according to your wishes after your passing.

Part 7: The Psychological Journey to Financial Freedom

- **Mindset Shifts:** This section explores the importance of developing a positive financial mindset, overcoming limiting beliefs, and staying motivated on your path to financial freedom.
- **Lifestyle Adjustments:** Learn how to adjust your lifestyle choices to align with your financial goals and embrace the benefits of a financially secure future.

Part 8: The Global Tiny House Phenomenon

- **Small Space, Big Dreams:** Tiny houses are typically defined as dwellings under 400 square feet (37 square meters). They come in a variety of styles, from trailers converted into cozy havens to architecturally designed wonders on wheels.
- **A Global Movement Takes Root:** The tiny house movement isn't confined to North America. Across the globe, people are finding ways to adapt the concept to their local contexts.

Part 9: The FIRE Movement
- **Escape the Hamster Wheel - The FIRE Movement:** The

Fire Formula, the Fire strategies and Variations of Fire
- **Beyond the Basics: A Deeper Dive into FIRE:** let's delve deeper into the practicalities and intricacies involved in achieving financial independence and early retirement.
- **Tailoring the Flame: Variations of the FIRE Movement:** This chapter explores some popular variations, allowing you to find the path that best suits your lifestyle and aspirations.
- **Stoking the FIRE: Practical Strategies for Success:** This chapter tackles the nitty-gritty – practical strategies to supercharge your savings, invest wisely, and build passive income streams that will propel you toward financial independence.
- **Navigating the Roadblocks: Challenges and Considerations on the FIRE Path:** This chapter explores the challenges you might encounter and offers resources to stay motivated and on track toward your goal of financial independence and early retirement.

- **The FIRE Within - A Conclusion and Call to Action:** The key takeaways and empower you to take charge of your financial future.

Part 10: Conclusion

- **Reaching Your Goals:** This section will provide guidance on navigating the journey to financial freedom, celebrating milestones, and adapting your strategies as needed.
- **Living a Fulfilling Life:** Financial freedom is not just about money, but about the freedom to pursue your passions and live a fulfilling life. Explore how to leverage your financial security to design a life you love.

Part 1: Building Your Financial Foundation

Chapter 1: Understanding Financial Freedom: Defining Your Dreamscape

Financial freedom is a powerful concept, often associated with early retirement, exotic vacations, and a life free from financial worries. While these are all potential benefits, the true essence of financial freedom is much more personal. This chapter will guide you in defining what financial freedom means for *you* and setting the foundation for your journey.

Different Flavors of Freedom

Financial freedom is not a one-size-fits-all concept. For some, it might be the ability to retire early and spend their days pursuing hobbies or traveling the world. Others might dream of starting a business they are passionate about, even if it means a non-traditional income stream. Still others might simply yearn for the peace of mind that comes with knowing their basic needs are covered, and they are not beholden to a demanding job.

It is important to identify what really matters to you. Ask yourself:

- What would I do with my time if I weren't limited by work?
- What experiences or goals are most important to me?
- What kind of lifestyle do I want to live in the future?

Understanding your desires and aspirations is the first step towards defining your unique path to financial freedom.

According to the organization ourworldindata.org, that tracked the working hours for the last 150 years concludes that working hours has reduced in some parts of the world, while many parts still work longer days and 6 to 7 days a week.

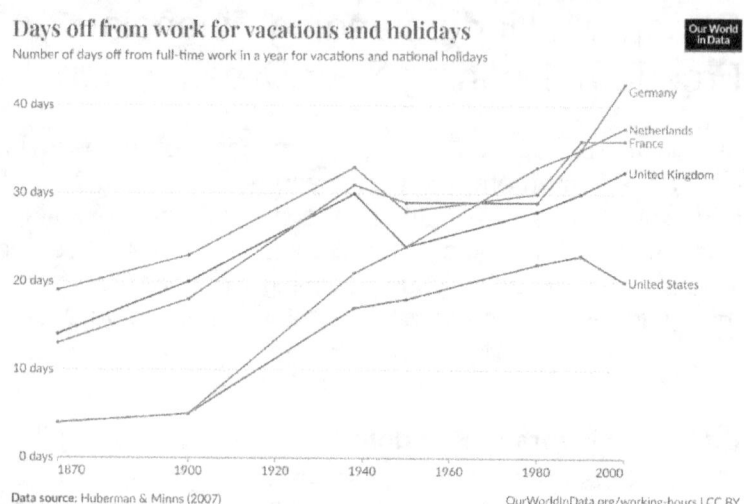

Numbers and Beyond

While achieving financial freedom does have a numerical component – the amount of passive income required to cover your living expenses – it's about more than just the numbers. Financial freedom is ultimately about having the freedom to choose how you spend your time and energy. It does not necessarily mean having an endless supply of cash to spend and having no reason to earn more.

Imagine your ideal day, week, or year. What activities would bring you joy and fulfillment? Would it involve travel, creative pursuits, spending time with loved ones, or simply the freedom to structure your day as you see fit?

By connecting your financial goals with your desired lifestyle, you can create a roadmap for achieving a freedom that goes beyond just having money in the bank.

Setting SMART Goals

Once you have a clearer vision of your financial freedom, it's time to translate it into actionable goals. SMART expands to:

- **Specific:** Instead of a vague desire for "more money," define exactly how much passive income you need per year to cover your desired lifestyle.
- **Measurable:** Establish clear benchmarks to track your progress. This could be a specific savings target per month or a desired investment portfolio value within a certain timeframe.
- **Achievable:** Be realistic about your goals and timeline. Consider your current income, earning potential, and risk tolerance when setting achievable targets.
- **Relevant:** Ensure your financial goals are aligned with your overall life goals and values.
- **Time-bound:** Set a specific timeframe for achieving your financial freedom goals. This will provide a sense of urgency and keep you motivated.

By setting SMART goals, you transform your dreamscape into a tangible roadmap for your financial journey.

Core Values Alignment

Financial freedom is not just about accumulating wealth; it's about empowering you to live a life that aligns with your core values. What truly matters to you? Is it financial security for your family? Experience of material possessions. Giving back to your community?

Understanding your core values will guide your financial decisions. For instance, if you value experiences over material possessions, you might be willing to downsize your living space or cut back on unnecessary spending to free up resources for travel or pursuing passions.

Aligning your financial goals with your core values ensures that achieving financial freedom leads to a life that feels truly fulfilling.

Lifestyle Evaluation

Before charting your course, it's essential to take a critical look at your current lifestyle. Understanding your spending habits and essential expenses will help determine the income level required to achieve your desired financial freedom.

Here are some key areas to consider:

- **Track your expenses:** For a month or two, meticulously track all your income and expenses. This will give a clear picture of where the money goes.
- **Differentiate needs from wants:** Identify your essential expenses – housing, food, utilities – and distinguish them from wants – dining out, entertainment, unnecessary subscriptions.
- **Identify areas for potential cuts:** Are there areas where you can realistically cut back on spending without sacrificing your well-being? Even small adjustments can free up significant resources over time.

By evaluating your current lifestyle and spending habits, you can determine the income gap that needs to be bridged to achieve financial freedom.

This chapter has hopefully shed light on the multifaceted nature of financial freedom. By identifying your personal aspirations, setting SMART goals, aligning your financial decisions with your core values, and evaluating your current lifestyle, you've taken the first crucial step towards defining your own unique path to financial freedom. The following chapters will delve deeper into the practical strategies and tools you can use to navigate this.

Anchor Point

The concept of financial freedom is more than just money. It's about having the freedom to choose how you spend your time and live a life that aligns with your values.

Chapter 2: Assessing Your Current Situation: Taking Stock for Takeoff

Imagine yourself embarking on a thrilling adventure. Before setting sail, a wise captain meticulously assesses their vessel – its strengths, weaknesses, and current course. Similarly, before embarking on your journey to financial freedom, it's crucial to assess your current financial situation. This chapter will equip you with the tools to take a clear and honest stock of your finances, providing a vital foundation for crafting your personalized roadmap.

Financial Snapshot: A Multifaceted View

A comprehensive financial snapshot goes beyond simply checking your bank balance. It involves a thorough examination of your income, expenses, debts, and assets. Here is what we'll delve into:

- **Income Streams:** Identify all sources of your income – salary, side hustle, rental income, investments. Knowing exactly how much money comes in each month is the first step towards effective budgeting and planning.
- **Expense Tracking:** Understanding where your money goes is essential. Utilize budgeting apps, spreadsheets, or simply a notebook to meticulously track your expenses for a month or two. Categorize your expenses into essentials (housing, food, utilities), discretionary spending (entertainment, dining out), and debt payments.

By tracking your expenses, you can identify areas for potential cuts and free up resources to accelerate your journey towards financial freedom.

- **Debt Inventory:** List all your debts – credit card balances, student loans, mortgages – including the outstanding balance, interest rate, and minimum monthly payment.

Having a clear picture of your debt situation will help you develop strategies for repayment and debt management.
- **Asset Valuation:** Take stock of your assets – your savings accounts, investment portfolios, retirement accounts, and even the value of your car or home. Knowing your net worth (assets minus liabilities) will provide a benchmark for measuring your progress over time. Companies like Credit Karma (as of 2023) offer this service for a small fee.

The Power of Awareness

Taking a comprehensive assessment of your current financial situation might reveal some surprises. You might discover hidden expenses you weren't aware of, or you might find areas where you can realistically cut back. The key takeaway is that **awareness is power**.

By having a clear understanding of your financial standing, you can make informed decisions about budgeting, saving, debt repayment, and investment strategies. This newfound awareness empowers you to take control of your financial future.

Embrace the Fresh Start Mentality

Don't be discouraged if your initial financial assessment reveals areas that need improvement. Maybe you drink a lot of coffee that adds up to a sizeable expenditure every month. Everyone starts somewhere, and the beauty of this journey is that you have the power to change your course.

View this assessment as a fresh start, an opportunity to gain clarity and make informed decisions about your financial future. Remember, **financial freedom is a marathon, not a sprint**. Be patient, celebrate small milestones, and use this assessment as a springboard to propel yourself forward.

The following chapters will provide you with practical tools and strategies for managing your expenses, tackling debt, building a budget, and saving for your future. By leveraging the knowledge gained from this financial assessment, you'll be well-equipped to navigate the path towards financial freedom.

Anchor Point

The importance of a comprehensive financial assessment before embarking on your journey to financial freedom. It emphasizes that a clear understanding of your income, expenses, debts, and assets is crucial for making informed decisions and crafting a personalized plan.

Chapter 3: Building a Budget and Tracking Expenses: Your Roadmap to Financial Freedom

You've assessed your financial situation, identified your goals, and are now ready to chart your course towards financial freedom. This chapter will equip you with two essential tools: creating a workable budget and diligently tracking your expenses. These tools will empower you to make informed financial decisions, allocate your resources effectively, and stay on track towards your goals.

Budgeting: Your Financial Roadmap

A budget is a roadmap, a plan that outlines how you intend to allocate your income towards your expenses and financial goals. While the specifics will vary depending on your unique situation, here's a framework for building your budget:

- **Categorize Your Expenses:** Divide your expenses into essential categories like housing, food, utilities, transportation, and debt payments. Then, allocate categories for discretionary spending like entertainment, dining out, and hobbies.
- **The 50/30/20 Rule (Optional):** This popular budgeting rule suggests allocating 50% of your income towards essential needs, 30% towards discretionary spending, and 20% towards savings and debt repayment. In my early days, I began a habit of making the first expenditure of the month as a savings. Move a manageable amount from your checking account to savings account. You can adjust this rule based on your specific circumstances.
- **Embrace Realistic Numbers:** Be honest with yourself about your spending habits. Don't underestimate expenses or overestimate your income.

Remember, your budget is a live document. You cannot define it once and forget. Review and adjust it regularly as your income or expenses change.

Expense Tracking: Staying on Course

Just like a pilot monitors their instruments to ensure they stay on course; expense tracking allows you to monitor your spending habits and ensure you're adhering to your budget. Here are some effective tracking methods:

- **Digital Tools:** Utilize budgeting apps or online spreadsheets to seamlessly track your income and expenses. Many tools offer automatic categorization and generate insightful reports. Banks began offering spending limits and alerts services. Take advantage of these features.
- **The Pen and Paper Method:** For a simpler approach, use a notebook to record your daily or weekly expenses. This method can be particularly helpful for those who prefer a hands-on approach.
- **Be Vigilant:** Track all your expenses, big or small, to get a complete picture of your spending habits. I used to set a link to a google form that I fill in my expenses immediately after my purchase is done. There are mobile apps that can scan a receipt and create a table. Make the best use of the available modern tools.

By religiously tracking expenses, you can identify areas where you might overspend and adjust your budget accordingly. Regular expense tracking also fosters accountability and helps you stay motivated on your journey.

The Power of the Budget-Expense Tracking Duo

Imagine a car with a well-defined destination (your budget) but no steering wheel (expense tracking). You might have a goal, but without the ability to course-correct, reaching your destination would be difficult. This is where the power of the budget-expense tracking duo comes in.

- **Making Informed Decisions:** The data gleaned from expense tracking empowers you to make informed financial decisions. For instance, if you see a high recurring expense on dining out, you can explore ways to cook more meals at home.
- **Identifying Leaks:** Expense tracking helps you identify areas where your money might be leaking out – forgotten subscriptions, impulse purchases. Plugging these leaks can free up resources for your financial goals.
- **Staying Motivated:** Seeing your progress towards your budget goals can be incredibly motivating. Tracking your spending allows you to celebrate milestones and visualize the progress you're making.

By combining a well-defined budget with consistent expense tracking, you gain control over your finances and empower yourself to navigate the path towards financial freedom. The following chapters will delve deeper into strategies for saving money, tackling debt, and building wealth through investments, all grounded in the foundation you've established with your budget and expense tracking system.

Anchor Point

The concept of budget and expense tracking working together as a system for financial control. The chapter uses the metaphor of a roadmap and steering wheel to illustrate that a budget provides direction (where you want to go with your money), and expense tracking allows you to monitor and adjust your spending (course correction) to stay on track towards your financial goals.

Part 2: Increasing Your Income

Chapter 4: Maximizing Your Current Income: Fueling Your Financial Freedom Journey

Your journey to financial freedom requires not just mindful spending but also a steady stream of income. This chapter will explore various strategies to maximize your income within your current job and introduce the concept of generating additional income streams.

Leveraging Your Current Role

Before venturing outside your current job, consider these strategies to potentially increase your income within your existing role:

- **Negotiate a Raise:** Research industry salary benchmarks for your position and experience level. If your performance merits it, prepare a data-driven case to negotiate a raise with your employer.
- **Seek Promotions:** Identify opportunities for advancement within your company. Discuss your career aspirations with your manager and demonstrate your commitment to take on additional responsibilities.
- **Develop In-Demand Skills:** Invest in acquiring new skills or certifications that are valuable in your industry. This can make you a more competitive candidate for promotions or higher-paying positions within your company.
- **Take on Additional Responsibilities:** Volunteer for challenging projects or express interest in taking on additional tasks. This demonstrates your initiative and could lead to increased compensation or pave the way for future promotions.

Remember: Communication is key. Schedule a meeting with your manager to discuss your career goals and explore possibilities for increased income within your current role.

Exploring Additional Income Streams

While maximizing your income within your current job is a great starting point, consider these additional income streams to accelerate your progress towards financial freedom:

- **Freelancing:** Leverage your existing skills to offer freelance services online or in your community. This could involve writing, editing, graphic design, consulting, or other skills you possess.
- **The Gig Economy:** Platforms like Uber, Lyft, AirBNB or DoorDash offer flexible opportunities to earn extra income on your own schedule. More business models are popping up every day. Take advantage of that.
- **Side Hustles:** Explore creative side hustles that align with your interests. This could involve selling crafts online, renting out a spare room, or starting a small blog. Or convert your hobby into an income stream. Are you a pilot? Start offering your expertise by teaching or flying delivering lifesaving essentials.

Remember, there's no one-size-fits-all approach. Choose an additional income stream that complements your current job, interests, and available time.

Building Your Earning Potential

Maximizing your current income and exploring additional income streams are not just about short-term gains. These efforts contribute to building your overall earning potential. Here's how:

- **Increased Value Proposition:** The skills and experience you gain from freelancing, side hustles, or additional

responsibilities within your current job make you a valuable asset. This strengthens your position when negotiating raises or promotions in the future.
- **Multiple Income Streams:** Having multiple income streams provides a financial safety net and reduces your reliance on a single source of income. This can be particularly beneficial in the event of job loss or economic downturns.
- **Investing Mindset:** The additional income you generate can be strategically invested to grow your wealth over time. This can significantly accelerate your progress towards achieving financial freedom.

By maximizing your current income and exploring additional streams, you're not just bringing in more money; you're investing in your future earning potential and building a solid foundation for financial freedom. The following chapters will delve deeper into strategies for saving your income, managing debt, and building wealth through various investment options.

Anchor Point

The concept of increasing your income as a strategy for achieving financial freedom. It explores two main approaches: maximizing your income within your current job and generating additional income streams.

Chapter 5: Developing Multiple Income Streams: Diversifying Your Path to Freedom

Financial freedom isn't just about how much you earn; it's about having a steady flow of income that comes in even when you're not actively working. This chapter will delve into the concept of multiple income streams, exploring various strategies to diversify your income sources and accelerate your journey to financial freedom.

Why Multiple Income Streams Matter

Imagine relying solely on a single stream – a river feeding your financial needs. If that river dries up due to job loss, economic downturns, or unexpected circumstances, you could face financial difficulties. Multiple income streams, on the other hand, function like a network of streams, ensuring a more constant flow of income even if one source dwindles.

Here are some key benefits of developing multiple income streams:

- **Financial Security:** Multiple income sources provide a safety net, mitigating the risk of relying solely on one job. Even if your main source of income experiences a setback, other streams can help you weather the storm.
- **Increased Earning Potential:** Each additional income stream contributes to your overall financial picture, accelerating your progress towards achieving your financial goals.
- **Freedom and Flexibility:** Having multiple income sources can provide greater control over your time and lifestyle. You might be able to work less at your primary job or pursue passions that wouldn't be financially viable with a single income stream.

Exploring Diverse Options

The beauty of multiple income streams lies in the variety of options available. Choose strategies that match your skills, interests, and available time. Here are some popular methods to consider:

- **Freelancing:** Leverage your existing skills to offer freelance services online or in your community. This could involve writing, editing, graphic design, consulting, or any skill you possess that others are willing to pay for. A home assessor is a great option.
- **The Gig Economy:** Platforms like Uber, Lyft, Doordash, and TaskRabbit offer flexible opportunities to earn extra income on your own schedule. These gigs can be a great way to utilize your free time productively.
- **Rental Income:** Renting out a spare room, your entire house while you're away, or even a storage space can generate passive income. This can be a particularly attractive option if you already own property.
- **Online Businesses:** Explore the world of e-commerce by selling products online through platforms like Etsy, Mercari, Shopify or your own website. You could also create and sell online courses, ebooks, or printables. In early 2024, Laser engraving devices have popped up to nurture one creativity.
- **Investing:** While not entirely passive (research and ongoing management are required), investments like stocks, bonds, or real estate can generate income through dividends, interest, or rental income. This chapter will delve deeper into investment strategies in later chapters.

Remember, there's no one-size-fits-all approach. The ideal combination of income streams will vary depending on your unique circumstances and goals.

Building Your Income Ecosystem

Think of your multiple income streams as parts of a well-functioning ecosystem. Here's how to strategically develop and manage them:

- **Identify Your Skills and Interests:** Capitalize on your existing skills and explore areas you're passionate about. This will make the process of building and maintaining your income streams more enjoyable and sustainable.
- **Start Small, Scale Gradually:** Don't overwhelm yourself by trying to launch multiple income streams simultaneously. Begin with one or two, and gradually add more as you gain experience and confidence.
- **Prioritize and Manage Time Effectively:** Balancing multiple income streams with your existing commitments requires effective time management. Prioritize tasks, create schedules, and delegate where possible.

By strategically developing and managing your income ecosystem, you'll create a robust financial foundation that fuels your journey towards financial freedom. The following chapters will explore strategies for saving your income, managing debt, and building wealth through various investment options. Remember, multiple income streams, coupled with wise financial management, can empower you to achieve your financial goals and unlock the doors to a life of freedom and security.

Anchor Point

The concept of multiple income streams as a strategy to achieve financial freedom. It emphasizes the importance of having a steady flow of income from various sources to mitigate risk, increase earning potential, and gain more control over your time and lifestyle.

Part 3: Living Frugally and Saving Wisely

Chapter 6: Adopting a Frugal Mindset: Mastering the Art of Intentional Spending

Financial freedom isn't about depriving yourself or living a life of austerity. It's about making conscious choices, prioritizing your goals, and getting the most value out of your hard-earned money. This chapter explores the concept of a frugal mindset, a powerful tool that will empower you to make informed spending decisions and accelerate your path to financial freedom.

Cambridge English dictionary describes "frugal" as: *careful when using money or food, or (of a meal) cheap or small in amount.* I grew up with water scarce therefore, my use of water is always frugal despite having access to abundant water. Frugal is not bad.

Beyond Tight Fists: The True Essence of Frugality

Frugality is often misconstrued as stinginess or deprivation. It's about intentionality. It's about **spending consciously**, prioritizing your needs over wants, and getting the most value out of your money.

Here's a shift in perspective:

- **From deprivation to mindful spending:** Instead of focusing on what you can't have, a frugal mindset empowers you to make conscious choices about where your money goes. You'll still enjoy life's pleasures, but you'll do so strategically, aligning your spending with your long-term goals.
- **From impulse buys to value-driven purchases:** Frugal living encourages you to question every purchase. Is this

item a need or a want? Does it offer lasting value, or is it a fleeting pleasure? This approach fosters a sense of intentionality and prevents impulse purchases that drain your finances.
- **From chasing trends to appreciating quality:** A frugal mindset doesn't mean sacrificing quality. Instead, it encourages you to seek out well-made, timeless items that will last. You might prioritize buying used items in good condition or invest in high-quality pieces that will serve you for years.

Shifting Your Spending Paradigm

Adopting a frugal mindset involves a shift in your spending paradigm. Here are some practical strategies to embrace:

- **Differentiate Needs from Wants:** Create a clear distinction between your essential needs – housing, food, utilities – and your wants – dining out, expensive vacations, entertainment. Focus on fulfilling your needs first, and then channel any remaining funds towards your wants, with a more conscious approach.
- **Embrace the Power of Budgeting:** As discussed in previous chapters, creating a budget is crucial. A well-defined budget allocates your income towards your needs and financial goals, leaving less room for impulsive spending.
- **Track Your Expenses:** Diligent expense tracking provides valuable insights into your spending habits. By identifying areas where you might be overspending, you can adjust your budget and make informed spending decisions.
- **Challenge Yourself to Save:** Set savings goals and employ creative strategies to achieve them. Consider a "no-spend weekend" challenge or explore ways to cut back on unnecessary expenses. Every dollar saved is a dollar invested in your future financial freedom.

Remember: Frugality is not about feeling deprived; it's about feeling empowered. By making conscious choices and prioritizing your goals, you'll gain control over your finances and unlock the doors to a future filled with financial security and freedom.

Frugal Living Doesn't Mean Sacrifice, It Means Freedom

The beauty of a frugal mindset lies in the freedom it grants you. Here's how:

- **Reduced Financial Stress:** By curbing unnecessary spending and prioritizing your financial goals, you'll experience less financial stress. This newfound peace of mind allows you to focus on what truly matters in life.
- **Greater Control Over Your Finances:** Frugal living empowers you to make informed financial decisions. You'll no longer be a slave to impulse buys or keeping up with the Joneses. Instead, you'll be in control of your money and your financial destiny.
- **Freedom to Pursue Your Passions:** When you're not burdened by excessive debt or frivolous spending, you'll have more resources to pursue your passions and interests. This could involve travel, hobbies, or even starting your own business.

By adopting a frugal mindset, you're not just saving money; you're investing in a future of freedom and possibility. The following chapters will explore strategies for tackling debt, saving for your future, and building wealth through various investment options. Remember, a frugal mindset coupled with sound financial planning will propel you towards your financial goals and unlock the doors to a life of freedom and fulfillment.

Anchor Point

The concept of a frugal mindset as a tool to achieve financial freedom. It clarifies that frugality is not about deprivation but rather about conscious spending, prioritizing needs over wants, and getting the most value out of your money. The passage emphasizes a shift in perspective from impulsive spending to mindful choices that align with your long-term financial goals.

Chapter 7: Debt Management: Conquering the Mountain on Your Path

Debt can feel like a heavy burden, a mountain looming on your path to financial freedom. This chapter equips you with the tools and strategies to effectively manage your debt, break free from its grip, and clear the way for a brighter financial future.

Understanding Your Debt Landscape

The first step towards conquering your debt mountain is taking a comprehensive inventory. Gather all your debt statements and categorize them based on the following:

- **Debt Type:** Differentiate between high-interest debt like credit cards and lower-interest debt like mortgages or student loans. High-interest debt should be prioritized for repayment due to the significant interest charges that accrue over time.
- **Interest Rates:** Knowing the interest rate on each debt helps you prioritize which ones to tackle first. Focus on paying down high-interest debt first to save money in the long run.
- **Minimum Payments:** List the minimum monthly payments required for each debt. This will help you understand your current debt obligations and identify areas where you can potentially free up additional resources for accelerated repayment.

By creating a clear picture of your debt landscape, you gain a realistic understanding of the challenge and can develop a targeted plan for repayment.

Debt Repayment Strategies: Climbing with

Confidence

Once you've mapped your debt mountain, it's time to choose your climbing route. Some of the effective debt repayment strategies to consider:

- **The Debt Avalanche:** This strategy focuses on paying down the debt with the highest interest rate first, regardless of the outstanding balance. By eliminating high-interest debt first, you save a significant amount of money in the long run.

  Example:
  Let's say you have two debts:
  - Credit Card A: Balance of $5,000 with an APR (Annual Percentage Rate) of 20%
  - Student Loan B: Balance of $10,000 with an APR of 5%

  The debt avalanche method would focus on paying off Credit Card A first, even though it has a smaller balance than the student loan. Here's why:
  - **High Interest:** The credit card has a much higher interest rate (20%) compared to the student loan (5%). This means the credit card is accumulating interest much faster, eating away at your payments. By paying it down first, you stop that high-cost interest from growing.
  - **Focus on Savings:** Every dollar you pay towards Credit Card A goes directly to reducing the principal balance and saving your money in interest. Even though the student loan has a larger balance, the lower interest rate makes it less urgent to tackle first.

  Here's a simplified example of how the payments might be allocated:
  - **Minimum Payments:** Let's say the minimum payment is $100 for each debt. You would continue making these minimum payments on both debts to stay current.
  - **Extra Payments:** If you have an extra $200 per

month for debt repayment, the debt avalanche method would focus all that extra money on Credit Card A.

By prioritizing the high-interest debt, you save money on interest charges in the long run. Once Credit Card A is paid off, you can then throw all your payments (minimum + extra) towards the student loan, eliminating it much faster.

- **The Debt Snowball:** This strategy prioritizes paying off the debt with the smallest balance first, regardless of interest rate. Seeing debts disappear quickly can be motivating and provide a sense of accomplishment, fostering continued progress.

Example:

Let's break down the debt snowball method using an example:

Imagine you have these three debts:
- Credit Card A: Balance of $1,000 with an APR of 18% (high interest)
- Medical Bill B: Balance of $500 with an APR of 10% (medium interest)
- Personal Loan C: Balance of $3,000 with an APR of 8% (low interest)

The debt snowball focuses on the smallest balance first, which is Medical Bill B ($500). Here's how it works:
- **Quick Wins:** You throw all your extra payments towards the medical bill. Let's say you have an extra $200 per month for debt repayment. You'd pay the $50 minimum payment and put the extra $150 towards the medical bill.
- **Psychological Boost:** Seeing the medical bill disappear quickly can be highly motivating. It gives you a sense of accomplishment and keeps you on track.
- **Tackling the Next One:** Once the medical bill is paid off, you roll that extra $150 you were paying towards it and add it to the minimum payment of Credit Card A. This increases your total payment on the credit card,

allowing you to pay it down faster.
Here's the key benefit:
- **Motivation Matters:** While the debt snowball might not save you the most money in interest compared to prioritizing high-interest debts, the psychological boost of seeing debts disappear can be crucial. It keeps you motivated and consistent with your debt repayment plan, ultimately helping you conquer all your debts.

Remember, this is a simplified example. The snowball method works best if you can consistently make extra payments towards the smallest balances. It's a great approach if you find satisfaction in achieving small milestones and staying motivated throughout the debt payoff journey.

- **Debt Consolidation:** Consider consolidating multiple debts with high-interest rates into a single loan with a lower interest rate. This can simplify your repayment process and potentially save you money in the long run. However, be cautious about extending repayment terms, as this could increase the total interest paid.

Example:
Let's see how debt consolidation can work with an example:
Imagine you have two credit cards with high interest rates:
- **Credit Card A:** Balance of $4,000 with an APR of 22%
- **Credit Card B:** Balance of $3,000 with an APR of 18%

You're making minimum payments on both cards, but it feels like you're barely making a dent. Here's how consolidation could help:
- **Debt Consolidation Loan**: You apply for a debt consolidation loan with a lower interest rate. Let's say you qualify for a loan of $7,000 at an APR of 12%.
- Pay Off Existing Debts: You would use the $7,000 loan to pay off the entire balances of both credit

cards. This eliminates the high-interest charges you were accruing each month.
- **Single Payment**: Now you only have one monthly payment to manage, for the consolidation loan. This simplifies your repayment process.

Potential Benefits:
- **Lower Interest:** With a lower interest rate (12% vs. 18-22%), you'd likely save money on interest charges in the long run.
- Simpler Management: One monthly payment is easier to track and manage compared to juggling multiple credit card bills.

Things to Consider:
- **Loan Terms**: Be mindful of the loan term (repayment period) offered for the consolidation loan. While a longer term might lower your monthly payment, it could also mean you pay more interest overall.
- **Credit Score Impact**: Applying for a new loan may cause a temporary dip in your credit score.

Financial institutions do offer a balance transfer facility with 12 to 15 months interest free. Take advantage of it.

The optimal strategy depends on your specific financial situation and risk tolerance. Evaluate your options and choose the approach that best suits your goals and personality.

Additional Tools in Your Debt-Fighting Arsenal

Beyond core repayment strategies, here are some additional tools to consider in your debt management journey:

- **Negotiate Lower Interest Rates:** Contact your creditors and attempt to negotiate lower interest rates on your existing debt accounts. Negotiate a commitment to

repayment and see if lenders agree to work with you.
- **Increase Your Income:** As discussed in previous chapters, exploring additional income streams can free up resources for faster debt repayment. Consider freelancing, side hustles, or a part-time job to generate extra income specifically for debt elimination.
- **Reduce Expenses:** Pair your debt repayment strategy with a commitment to frugal living. By cutting back on unnecessary expenses, you can allocate more resources towards tackling your debt.

Remember, debt management is a marathon, not a sprint. Be patient, celebrate milestones, and stay committed to your repayment plan. The following chapters will delve into strategies for saving for your future and building wealth through various investment options. Conquering your debt mountain will free up resources and empower you to pursue your long-term financial goals with greater confidence.

Anchor Point

The concept of debt repayment strategies as a tool to clear the path towards financial freedom. The passage starts by emphasizing the importance of understanding your debt landscape (types, interest rates, minimum payments) before diving into different repayment strategies like debt avalanche, debt snowball, and debt consolidation. The chapter acknowledges that the best strategy depends on your specific situation and emphasizes the importance of additional tools like negotiation, increasing income, and reducing expenses to pay off debt faster.

Chapter 8: Saving Strategies: Building Your Financial Springboard

Debt management is crucial, but it's only half the equation. Financial freedom also requires building a solid foundation of savings. This chapter explores various saving strategies to help you accumulate the resources needed to achieve your financial goals.

Identifying Your Savings Goals

The first step is to identify your specific savings goals. Here are some common categories to consider:

- **Emergency Fund:** Aim to save 3-6 months' worth of living expenses in a readily accessible account to cover unexpected emergencies like job loss or medical bills.
- **Short-Term Goals:** Do you have a dream vacation or a down payment on a car in mind? Create a savings target and timeline for these short-term goals.
- **Long-Term Goals:** Retirement might seem far off, but starting early is key. Set savings goals for your retirement and explore investment options for long-term wealth creation.

Having clearly defined goals provides direction and motivation for your saving efforts.

Building Your Savings Arsenal

There's no one-size-fits-all approach to saving. Here are some strategies to consider:

- **Automate Savings:** Like I mentioned earlier, let your first expense after a paycheck be moving a small amount to

savings account. This "pay yourself first" approach ensures you prioritize saving before you even see the money.
- **The 52-Week Challenge:** This fun strategy involves saving a set amount each week – starting with $1 and increasing by $1 each week. By the end of the year, you'll have saved a significant sum.
- **Utilize Multiple Savings Accounts:** Consider opening separate accounts for different goals. A high-yield savings account might be ideal for your emergency fund, while a retirement account like an IRA can offer tax advantages for long-term savings.
- **Embrace the Power of "No-Spend" Days/Weeks:** Challenge yourself to spend less or nothing on specific days or weeks. This can help you free up additional resources for savings and curb impulse spending.

Experiment with different strategies, find what works best for you, and be consistent with your efforts.

Prioritizing Savings: Overcoming Obstacles

Let's be honest, saving isn't always easy. Tips to overcome common obstacles:

- **Temptation Busters:** Identify situations that trigger impulse spending. Avoid malls or online shopping sprees if you know they weaken your resolve. Avoid browsing through food section when hungry.
- **Track Your Progress:** Seeing your savings grow can be incredibly motivating. Track your progress towards your goals and celebrate milestones to stay on track.
- **Reframe Your Mindset:** Instead of viewing saving as deprivation, focus on the freedom and security it provides. Think about the peace of mind a well-funded emergency fund or a comfortable retirement will bring.

Remember, consistent saving, even in small amounts, can

accumulate significantly over time. The power of compound interest will work in your favor, turning your savings into a formidable springboard towards financial freedom.

Living Below Your Means: The Cornerstone of Saving

The key to successful saving lies in living below your means. This means spending less than you earn and consistently allocating a portion of your income towards savings. Here are some practical tips:

- **Review Your Budget:** Revisit your budget regularly and identify areas where you can cut back on spending.
- **Embrace Frugal Living:** As discussed in Chapter 6, adopting a frugal mindset empowers you to prioritize needs over wants and get the most value out of your money. This naturally translates into increased savings.
- **Evaluate Recurring Expenses:** Audit your monthly subscriptions and recurring expenses. Service providers often run deals. Negotiate lower rates where possible. These small adjustments can free up significant resources for savings.

By consistently living below your means and prioritizing saving, you'll build a solid financial foundation and empower yourself to pursue your financial goals with confidence. The following chapters will delve into building wealth through various investment options, strategies for long-term financial growth, and navigating your path towards financial freedom.

Anchor Point

The concept of building a savings foundation is a crucial step towards financial freedom. The passage emphasizes the importance of setting clear savings goals (emergency fund, short-term goals, long-term goals) and explores various strategies to achieve them. These strategies include automating savings, utilizing different accounts, embracing "no-spend" challenges, and prioritizing living below your means. The chapter highlights the power of consistent saving and compound interest in reaching your financial goals.

Part 4: Investing for Growth

Chapter 9: Understanding Investments: Growing Your Wealth for the Long Term

You've tackled your debt, built a solid savings foundation, and are now ready to explore the exciting world of investing. This chapter will equip you with the basic knowledge and strategies to confidently navigate the investment landscape and grow your wealth for the long term.

Investing: From Seed to Harvest

Think of investing like planting a seed. You invest your money (the seed) in various assets with the expectation that it will grow over time (the harvest), generating returns and building your wealth. While there's always some risk involved, investing is a powerful tool for achieving your long-term financial goals, such as a comfortable retirement or early financial freedom.

Investment Fundamentals: Building Your Knowledge Base

Before diving into specific investment options, it's crucial to grasp some fundamental concepts:

- **Risk and Return:** Generally, higher potential returns come with higher risk. Understanding your risk tolerance is essential. Are you comfortable with short-term fluctuations for potentially high long-term gains, or do you prefer a more conservative approach?
- **Diversification:** Spread your investments across different asset classes like stocks, Mutual Funds, ETF, bonds, and real estate to mitigate risk. Make sure you understand margin accounts before unleashing it.
- **Time Horizon:** Investing is a marathon, not a sprint.

Consider your investment timeline. What's your financial horizon? Are you looking to achieve a goal in the next few years, like a vacation or a car, a boat or are you focused on building wealth for the long term, like retirement? Your time horizon will influence your investment choices.

By understanding these fundamentals, you'll be well-equipped to make informed investment decisions.

Exploring the Investment Landscape: A Wealth of Options

The investment world offers a variety of options to suit your risk tolerance and goals. Here's a glimpse into some popular asset classes:

- **Stocks:** Owning shares in companies allows you to participate in their growth. Stocks may offer high returns, but they are also riskier. Spend good time educating yourselves before trading. We spend 12 to 16 years in education before starting to work. Trading is similar, investing in education.
- **Bonds:** Essentially, you loan money to a government or corporation in exchange for regular interest payments. Depending upon the time, bonds may be considered less risky than stocks but also offer lower potential returns. Types of bonds are Government Bonds, Corporate Bonds, Mortgage-backed securities and savings bonds. Please do your research before venturing into them.
- **Treasury Bills:** Treasury bills (T-bills) are short-term U.S. government debt investments with maturities between four weeks and one year. They are sold at a discount, meaning you earn a return by the difference between the purchase price and the face value received at maturity. Considered very safe due to U.S. government backing, they offer lower returns compared to riskier investments.
- **Mutual Funds and ETFs:** These are professionally

managed investment vehicles that pool money from multiple investors and invest in a variety of assets. This provides instant diversification and reduces risk compared to investing in individual stocks.
- **Real Estate:** Investing in rental properties can generate passive income through rent and potential appreciation in property value. However, real estate requires ongoing management and comes with its own set of risks.
- **Precious Metals:** Trading precious metals involves short-term bets on price movements. You'll need to analyze charts and market trends to capitalize on these fluctuations. This approach is risky and requires significant knowledge to manage the ups and downs of the market, but it can potentially deliver quick profits.
- **Commodity:** Commodity trading involves buying and selling contracts based on raw materials like oil, gold, or wheat. Traders aim to profit from price swings by analyzing supply, demand, and global events. This is a fast-paced and risky market, but successful trades can lead to high returns.

REITs, or Real Estate Investment Trusts, allow you to invest in income-producing real estate without the burden of directly buying and managing properties. These companies own and operate a variety of buildings, from apartment complexes and offices to healthcare facilities and shopping centers. By investing in REITs on major stock exchanges, you can gain access to this market like buying stocks. They offer the potential for regular income through dividend payouts, and the chance for your investment to grow over time through rising share prices. Plus, REITs can diversify your portfolio by providing exposure to real estate without the complexities of property management.

Trading vs Investing in Precious Metals

Trading

- **Goal**: Short-term profits by capitalizing on price fluctuations.
- **Time Horizon**: Short-term, could be minutes, hours, days, or weeks.
- **Strategies**: Traders use technical analysis like charts and indicators to identify buying and selling opportunities based on price movements, supply and demand, and market sentiment.
- **Risk**: High risk due to the volatile nature of precious metal prices. Requires significant knowledge and experience to manage risk effectively.
- **Examples**: Buying and selling futures contracts, CFDs (contracts for difference), or margin trading precious metals.

Investing

- **Goal**: Long-term wealth preservation or growth by holding precious metals for their intrinsic value.
- **Time Horizon**: Long-term, could be years or even decades.
- **Strategies**: Investors might buy physical precious metals like coins or bars, invest in ETFs (exchange-traded funds) that track precious metal prices, or buy stocks of mining companies. Focuses on holding the asset through market fluctuations.
- **Risk**: Lower risk than trading, but precious metal prices can still be volatile in the long run.
- **Examples**: Buying gold bars, investing in a gold ETF, or buying shares in a gold mining company.

Remember, this is just a brief overview. Conduct thorough research before investing in any specific asset class.

Investment Strategies for Different Goals

The investment strategy you choose will depend on your specific goals and risk tolerance. Here are some general guidelines:

- **Growth for Long-Term Goals:** For long-term goals like retirement, a growth-oriented strategy might be suitable. This could involve investing in a mix of stocks and stock funds that offer the potential for higher returns over time.
- **Income for Short-Term Goals:** If you're saving for a short-term goal like a down payment on a house, you might prioritize income-generating investments like bonds or dividend-paying stocks.
- **Balancing Risk and Return:** The key lies in finding a balance between risk and return that aligns with your comfort level and goals. A diversified portfolio with a mix of asset classes can help achieve this balance.

Day Trading

Day trading is an active investment strategy in the stock market focused on short-term profits. Here's the key idea:

- **Rapid Buying and Selling:** Day traders buy and sell stocks (or other assets) within the same trading day, sometimes multiple times. They aim to capitalize on small price fluctuations throughout the day.
- **Focus on Price Movement:** Unlike long-term investors who research company fundamentals, day traders primarily focus on technical analysis of price charts and trading patterns.
- **High Risk, High Reward:** Day trading can be profitable, but it also carries significant risk. The fast-paced nature and frequent transactions require constant attention, discipline, and a strong understanding of the market.

Day trading, while potentially lucrative, is fraught with risk. The constant buying and selling, coupled with the need for intense focus and experience, makes it a challenging path towards profit.

Trading Stock Options

Stock options are essentially contracts that grant you the right, not the obligation, to buy or sell a stock at a specific price by a specific date. Like a reservation for a stock purchase, they offer leverage, letting you control more shares with less money upfront than buying the stock itself. There are two main types: calls for buying the stock if you think it will go up (bullish) and puts to sell it if you think it will go down (bearish). However, options are complex and can be risky, so be sure to understand them well before starting to trade.

- **Covered Call:** Sell a call option on a stock you already own, collecting income but limiting potential gains if the stock price rises significantly.
- **Cash-Secured Put:** You sell a put option and collect cash up front but are obligated to buy the stock if the price falls below a certain level (like a bet the price will stay high).
- **Credit Spread:** Earn a profit by selling an option at a higher strike price and buying an option at a lower strike price (both calls or both puts). You profit if the price stays flat or moves in your favor (a little).
- **Iron Condor:** Limits your risk by selling a bull put spread (selling a put at a lower price and buying a put at a higher price) and a bear call spread (selling a call at a higher price and buying a call at a lower price) together. You profit if the stock price stays within a certain range.

- **Butterfly Spread:** Like a credit spread, but you use three options at different strike prices to limit your risk and potential profit.
- **Iron Butterfly:** Combines a bull put butterfly and a bear call butterfly, limiting your risk on price movements in either direction.
- **Short Straddle:** Sell both a call and put option at the same strike price. You profit if the stock price stays flat (high risk, as price movements hurt you).
- **Calendar Spread (Time Spread):** Buy an option with a longer expiration (giving you more time) and sell an option with a shorter expiration (same type, call or put). You benefit from a price move but need time for it to happen.
- **Diagonal Spread:** Like a calendar spread but uses options with different expiration dates and strike prices for more flexibility.
- **Box Spread:** A combination of four options at different strike prices to profit from a limited price movement in the stock.
- **Long Straddle:** Buy both a call and put option at the same strike price and expiration, profiting if the stock price moves significantly in either direction (high risk).
- **Short Straddle:** Sell both a call and put option at the same strike price, profiting if the stock price stays flat (high risk). This is the opposite of a long straddle.
- **Bull Call Spread):** Buy a lower strike call and sell a higher strike call, benefiting from a moderate increase in the stock price with limited risk and reward.
- **Bull Put Spread:** Buy a lower strike put and sell a higher strike put, profiting if the stock price stays flat or increases slightly. Limit your risk and reward.
- **Synthetic Call:** Combine buying a stock and a put option to mimic owning a call option.

- **Protective Put:** Buy a put option on a stock you already own as insurance in case the price falls. Limits your downside risk.
- **Bear Call Spread:** Sell a lower strike call and buy a higher strike call, profiting if the stock price falls or stays flat. Limit your risk and reward.
- **Strip:** Sell all the put options at a certain expiration date for a stock.
- **Synthetic Put:** Combine buying a put option and selling a stock to mimic owning a put option.
- **Married Put:** Like a protective put, but you buy a put option with a strike price lower than your purchase price of the stock.
- **Long Put:** Buy a put option, giving you the right to sell a stock at a certain price by a certain date. You profit if the stock price falls.
- **Call Ratio Spread:** Sell multiple call options and buy one call option at different strike prices.
- **Put Ratio Spread:** Sell multiple put options and buy one put option at different strike prices.
- **Protective Collar:** Combine selling a covered call with buying a protective put, limiting your risk in both up and down movements.
- **Ratio Call Backspread:** Buy a call option and sell two call options at different strike prices.
- **Ratio Put Backspread:** Buy a put option and sell two put options at different strike prices.
- **Collar Spread:** Like a protective collar, but with different expiration dates for the call and put options.

Remember, these are simplified explanations, and options trading can be complex. It's important to consult with a financial advisor before starting.

Seeking Professional Guidance

The world of trading and investing can be complex. Consider consulting with a licensed financial advisor for personalized advice tailored to your specific financial situation and goals. A financial advisor can help you develop an investment strategy, choose suitable investment vehicles, and manage your portfolio over time.

By understanding the fundamentals of investing, exploring various options, and aligning your strategy with your goals, you'll be well on your way to growing your wealth and achieving financial freedom. The following chapters will delve into additional considerations like asset allocation, investment fees, and navigating the stock market to empower you on your investment journey.

Anchor Point

The anchor point of this chapter is **investing for the long term**. The chapter uses the metaphor of planting a seed to illustrate this concept. It emphasizes the importance of understanding risk tolerance, time horizon, and diversification to make informed investment decisions and achieve long-term financial goals. While the chapter explores various investment options and strategies, it circles back to the core idea of investing for the long term throughout the discussion.

Chapter 10: Developing an Investment Strategy: Your Personalized Roadmap to Wealth Creation

Now that you've grasped the investment landscape, it's time to craft your personalized roadmap to wealth creation. This chapter will guide you through the process of developing a solid investment strategy that aligns with your goals, risk tolerance, and financial situation.

Understanding Your Investment Persona

Before diving into specific asset allocations, take some time for introspection. Consider these factors to define your investment persona:

- **Risk Tolerance:** How comfortable are you with potential losses? Are you willing to accept short-term fluctuations for higher potential returns, or do you prefer a more conservative approach with lower risk?
- **Investment Goals:** What are you saving for? Pay off your house, a child's education, or a dream vacation? Your goals will influence your time horizon and risk tolerance.
- **Investment Time Horizon:** When do you need to access your invested funds? Long-term goals allow for a more aggressive strategy compared to short-term goals, which might necessitate a more conservative approach.
- **Financial Knowledge and Experience:** Are you a seasoned investor or just starting out? Your level of comfort with managing investments will influence your strategy.

Understanding your investment persona forms the foundation for crafting a personalized and sustainable investment strategy.

Building Your Investment Portfolio: A Balanced Approach

Think of your investment portfolio as a well-diversified ecosystem. Here's how to construct a balanced portfolio that aligns with your risk tolerance and goals:

- **Asset Allocation:** This refers to the distribution of your investments across different asset classes like stocks, bonds, real estate, and cash equivalents. A young investor with a long-time horizon might allocate a higher percentage to stocks for growth potential, while a retiree nearing their golden years might prioritize bonds for income and stability.
- **Diversification is Key:** Don't put all your eggs in one basket. Spread your investments across different asset classes and within each class (e.g., various sectors within stocks) to mitigate risk. A diversified portfolio is less susceptible to market fluctuations in any single sector.
- **Rebalancing Regularly:** Over time, the value of your investments will fluctuate. Learn to rebalance your portfolio based on market trends or personal situation. For instance, when the economy is slowing down, move your equity-based assets to more dividend-based stocks. Or when you hit a magic number of 50 years, go less aggressive. This might involve buying or selling assets to ensure your portfolio stays aligned with your risk tolerance and goals.

Remember, there's no one-size-fits-all allocation strategy. Do your research and consider seeking professional advice to determine the optimal asset allocation for your unique situation.

Beyond Asset Allocation: Additional Considerations

While asset allocation is a cornerstone of a sound investment strategy, here are some additional factors to consider:

- **Investment Fees:** Mutual funds, ETFs, and some managed accounts come with fees. Understanding and minimizing these fees is crucial to maximize your long-term returns.
- **Tax Implications:** Different investment vehicles have varying tax implications. Research tax-advantaged accounts like IRAs or 401(k)s to maximize your returns by minimizing taxes.
- **Investment Time Horizon:** The closer you are to your goals, the more conservative your investment strategy should become. Consider gradually shifting your portfolio towards less volatile assets as your time horizon shortens.

(**Exchange-traded funds (ETFs)** are like investment baskets you buy and sell on a stock exchange, just like a single stock. They hold a collection of assets, often stocks, bonds, or a mix, which track a particular market index or investment strategy. This allows you to diversify your holdings and potentially gain exposure to a whole sector of the market with a single purchase. ETFs trade throughout the day, like stocks, and offer various advantages like affordability, diversification, and ease of trading.)

By incorporating these additional considerations, you'll craft a comprehensive and well-rounded investment strategy.

Investing is a Marathon, not a Sprint: Discipline and Patience

Remember, successful investing is a long-term endeavor. Don't expect to get rich quickly. Develop a disciplined approach, invest consistently, and remain patient. Markets will fluctuate, but by staying focused on your long-term goals and rebalancing regularly, you'll be well-positioned to weather the storms and reap the rewards of your investment journey.

The following chapters will delve deeper into specific investment options, navigating the stock market, and additional strategies for wealth creation. With a sound investment strategy in place, you'll be empowered to take control of your financial future and unlock your path to financial freedom.

Anchor Point

The anchor point of this chapter is **building a personalized investment strategy**.

The chapter focuses on guiding you through the process of creating an investment plan that aligns with your individual risk tolerance, financial goals, and investment time horizon. It emphasizes **understanding your investment persona** as the foundation for this strategy.

While the chapter covers various aspects of portfolio construction and investment management, it consistently circles back to the core idea of developing a personalized and sustainable investment strategy.

Chapter 11: Building Long-Term Wealth: Cultivating Habits for Financial Freedom

Financial freedom isn't a destination; it's a journey. This chapter will explore the core principles and habits you can cultivate to build long-term wealth and secure your financial future.

Beyond the Numbers: The Mindset Shift

Building long-term wealth is less about a single magic bullet and more about cultivating a mindful approach towards money management. Here's a shift in perspective:

- **From Short-Term Gratification to Long-Term Goals:** Focus on delayed gratification. Prioritize saving and investing over impulsive spending. Keep your long-term goals in mind and make financial decisions that align with achieving them.
- **From Keeping Up with the Joneses to Financial Independence:** Comparison is the thief of joy, and financial security. Focus on your own financial journey, not keeping up with others. Build wealth at your own pace, prioritizing your financial well-being.
- **From Fear-Based Decisions to Informed Action:** Educate yourself about personal finance. The more you understand about investing, budgeting, and wealth management, the more confident you'll be in making informed financial decisions.

By adopting a long-term perspective and prioritizing your financial well-being, you'll lay a solid foundation for building wealth.

The Pillars of Wealth Building: Habits for

Success

Building long-term wealth requires consistent effort and dedication. Here are some habits to cultivate:

- **Live Below Your Means:** This principle forms the bedrock of wealth creation. Spend less than you earn and consistently allocate a portion of your income towards savings and investments.
- **Embrace Frugal Living:** As discussed in Chapter 6, adopting a frugal mindset empowers you to prioritize your needs over wants and get the most value out of your money. This naturally translates into increased savings and resources for investment.
- **Automate Your Finances:** Set up automatic transfers from your checking account to your savings and investment accounts. This "pay yourself first" approach ensures you prioritize saving and investing before you even see the money.
- **Invest Consistently:** Time is a powerful ally in wealth creation. Start small and investing early and increase your contributions as your income grows. The power of compound interest will work in your favor, turning your savings into a significant sum over time. Stockbrokers now offer fractional purchases as well. Utilize it.
- **Continuously Educate Yourself:** The world of finance is constantly evolving. Stay up to date on investment strategies, market trends, and tax regulations. The more you know, the better equipped you'll be to make informed investment decisions.
- **Seek Professional Guidance (Optional):** Consider consulting with a financial advisor for personalized advice tailored to your specific financial situation and goals. They can help you develop an investment strategy, choose suitable investment vehicles, and manage your portfolio over time.

Here are some key stock trading terms to know:
- **Order Types:** These specify how you want to buy or

sell a stock. Common types include market orders (buy/sell at current price) and limit orders (buy/sell at a specific price or better).
- **Bid-Ask Spread:** The difference between the highest price a buyer is willing to pay (bid) and the lowest price a seller is willing to accept (ask) for a stock.
- **Bull vs. Bear Market:** A bull market is a period of rising stock prices, while a bear market is a period of falling stock prices.
- **Volatility:** A measure of how much the price of a stock fluctuates over time.
- **Liquidity:** How easily a stock can be bought or sold without affecting the price significantly.
- **Dividend:** A portion of a company's profits that is distributed to shareholders.
- **Earnings per Share (EPS):** A measure of a company's profit per share of outstanding stock.
- **Market Capitalization:** The total market value of a company's outstanding shares.
- **Margin:** Borrowing money from a broker to buy stocks. This can magnify gains but also losses.
- **Portfolio:** The collection of investments you hold.

These habits, coupled with a disciplined approach, will propel you on your wealth-building journey.

Patience and Discipline: Your Guiding Lights

Building long-term wealth requires patience and discipline. Markets will fluctuate, and there will be periods of temptation to stray from your plan. Here's how to stay on track:

- **Develop a Long-Term Perspective:** Focus on the long game. Don't get discouraged by short-term market fluctuations. Stay invested and trust your strategy to deliver results over time.
- **Rebalance Regularly:** As discussed in Chapter 10, rebalance your portfolio periodically to maintain your

desired asset allocation. This ensures your risk tolerance and investment goals remain aligned.
- **Minimize Emotional Investing:** Don't let emotions dictate your investment decisions. Fear and greed are often the enemies of sound investing. Stick to your investment strategy and avoid making impulsive decisions based on market movements.

By maintaining a long-term perspective, practicing discipline, and remaining patient, you'll be well-positioned to navigate the inevitable ups and downs of the market and achieve your long-term wealth-building goals.

Building Long-Term Wealth: The Key to Freedom

Financial freedom isn't just about having a lot of money; it's about having control over your financial future. By cultivating the habits and strategies outlined in this chapter, you'll be empowered to:

- **Pursue Your Passions:** Financial freedom allows you to pursue your passions and interests without being restricted by financial limitations.
- **Reduce Financial Stress:** Knowing you have a secure financial future significantly reduces stress and anxiety, allowing you to live a more fulfilling life.
- **Leave a Legacy:** Building wealth allows you to plan and potentially leave a legacy for your loved ones.

Building long-term wealth is a journey of self-discovery, discipline, and continuous learning.

Anchor Point

The anchor point of this chapter is **cultivating habits for building long-term wealth**.

The chapter emphasizes that financial freedom is a journey, and achieving it requires a mindset shift and consistent effort. It outlines the core principles and habits you can develop to secure your financial future, focusing on the importance of:
- **Living below your means and embracing frugality**
- **Automating your finances and investing consistently**
- **Continuously educating yourself about personal finance**
- **Maintaining a long-term perspective and staying disciplined**

The chapter acknowledges seeking professional guidance as an option but focuses on the core idea that you can take control of your financial future by cultivating these habits.

Chapter 12: Understand the world of Cryptocurrency

Imagine it's 2008. The financial crisis is like a giant video game glitch - banks are crashing, people are losing money, and trust in the system is shaky. Enter Satoshi Nakamoto, a mysterious person (or maybe even a group of people!), who decides the world needs a new kind of money.

Forget coins and bills, this is digital cash – but not like anything you've seen before. Satoshi invented Bitcoin, a super secure system where money isn't controlled by any bank or government. It's like a giant public ledger everyone can see, but no one can mess with.

Here's the cool part: there's no giant printing press cranking out endless Bitcoins. Instead, powerful computers all over the world race to solve complex puzzles, and whoever wins gets rewarded with a brand-new Bitcoin. This process is called "mining" – like mining for gold, but instead of digging in dirt, you're using computer power.

Since there's a limited number of Bitcoins ever going to be created (around 21 million!), the idea is that they'll become more valuable over time, kind of like rare baseball cards.

Of course, it wasn't all smooth sailing. At first, only a handful of tech geeks knew about Bitcoin. They used it to buy things like pizza (the first Bitcoin purchase ever was for two Papa John's pizzas!). But slowly, more and more people started to see the potential.

Today, Bitcoin is a worldwide phenomenon. It's a bit of a wild ride – its value can go up and down faster than a rollercoaster. But whether you see it as the future of money or a giant digital mystery, there's no denying Bitcoin's a fascinating invention that came about in a time of crisis.

Welcome to the exciting and sometimes perplexing world of cryptocurrency! This chapter serves as your guide to understanding the basics of the crypto market, its core components, and the way it functions.

What is Cryptocurrency?

Imagine a digital payment system that doesn't rely on banks or governments. That's the core idea behind cryptocurrency. It's a digital asset designed to work as a medium of exchange, utilizing cryptography for security. Unlike traditional currencies, crypto exists solely as a record of ownership on a digital ledger called a blockchain.

Key Features of Cryptocurrencies:

- **Decentralization:** Cryptocurrencies operate on a decentralized network, meaning no single authority controls them. Transactions are verified and recorded by a network of computers around the world.
- **Security:** Cryptography secures crypto transactions, making them tamper-proof and verifiable.
- **Transparency:** All transactions are recorded publicly on the blockchain, ensuring transparency.

Where Does Crypto Trade?

Cryptocurrencies are traded on online platforms called cryptocurrency exchanges. These exchanges function like stock exchanges, allowing users to buy, sell, and trade cryptocurrencies.

Types of Cryptocurrencies:

- **Bitcoin:** The first and most famous cryptocurrency, known for its innovative blockchain technology.
- **Altcoins:** Alternative cryptocurrencies offering different features or functionalities than Bitcoin. Thousands of altcoins exist, each with its own purpose.
- **Stablecoins:** Cryptocurrencies pegged to a stable asset, like the US dollar, to reduce price volatility.

Understanding Crypto Market Terminology:

- **Market Capitalization:** The total market value of all outstanding units of a cryptocurrency.
- **Volatility:** The extent to which the price of a cryptocurrency fluctuates over time. Crypto markets are known for their high volatility.

- **Mining:** The process of creating new units of cryptocurrency by solving complex mathematical problems.
- **Wallet:** A digital wallet stores your cryptocurrency holdings securely.

Benefits and Risks of Cryptocurrencies:

Benefits:
- Decentralization and independence from traditional financial systems.
- Potential for high returns (although also high risk).
- Secure and transparent transactions.

Risks:
- High volatility can lead to significant losses.
- Unregulated market susceptible to fraud and scams.
- Complex technology with a learning curve for new users.

This chapter provides a foundational understanding of the crypto market. In the next chapter, we'll delve deeper into the inner workings of this dynamic and ever-evolving landscape.

Navigating the NFT Marketplace

The world of digital assets has exploded in popularity, and NFTs (Non-Fungible Tokens) are at the forefront of this revolution. This chapter serves as your compass for navigating the NFT marketplace, exploring its core concepts, functionalities, and the exciting possibilities it presents.

Demystifying NFTs

Imagine a unique digital certificate of ownership for a virtual item, like artwork, music, or even a tweet. That's the essence of an NFT. It leverages blockchain technology to verify the authenticity and ownership of digital assets, transforming them into collectible items in the digital realm.

What Makes NFTs Special?

- **Uniqueness:** Each NFT is one-of-a-kind, unlike fungible tokens (like cryptocurrencies) where one unit is identical to another.
- **Ownership:** Owning an NFT grants you demonstrable proof of ownership for the digital asset.
- **Security:** Blockchain technology ensures secure recording and verification of ownership history.

Where are NFTs Traded?

NFTs are primarily bought and sold on online marketplaces dedicated to digital assets. These platforms connect creators (artists, musicians, etc.) with collectors and provide a space for NFT discovery, bidding, and ownership transfer.

Exploring Different Types of NFTs

The NFT landscape is brimming with creativity. Here are some popular NFT categories:

- **Digital Art:** Paintings, illustrations, and other artistic creations in digital format.
- **Collectibles:** Trading cards, sports memorabilia, and other digital collectibles.
- **Gaming Items:** In-game assets, avatars, or virtual land within online games.
- **Music & Video:** Exclusive song rights, music videos, or behind-the-scenes content.
- **Real-World Assets:** Tokenized ownership or representation of physical assets like real estate.

Key Considerations Before Entering the NFT Market

- **Understanding Value:** The value of an NFT is subjective and depends on factors like creator reputation, utility, and overall market demand.
- **Transaction Fees:** Buying or selling NFTs often involves blockchain transaction fees (gas fees) that can be significant.
- **Environmental Impact:** The energy consumption of some blockchains used for NFTs has raised environmental concerns.

The Potential of NFTs

NFTs offer a revolutionary way to own and monetize digital creations. They empower creators to connect directly with audiences and establish new revenue streams. Additionally, NFTs have the potential to reshape ownership models for various digital assets and collectibles.

The Future of the NFT Market

The NFT market is still young and evolving rapidly. As technology advances and regulations develop, we can expect NFTs to integrate further into mainstream culture and redefine digital ownership.

This chapter equips you with the foundational knowledge to explore the NFT marketplace with more confidence. Remember, the NFT space is dynamic and staying informed is crucial for navigating its ever-changing landscape.

Anchor Point

The traditional financial system (banks, governments) serves as the anchor point. Bitcoin is presented as a completely new way to think about money, breaking free from the limitations of the existing system.

Part 5: Building Passive Income Streams

Part 5: Building Passive Income Streams

Chapter 13: Rental Properties: Building Wealth Through Bricks and Mortar

Real estate investing, particularly through rental properties, can be a compelling path to building wealth and generating passive income. This chapter explores the intricacies of becoming a landlord, the potential benefits and drawbacks of rental properties, and strategies to navigate this exciting yet demanding investment avenue.

The Allure of Rental Properties: Income and Appreciation

Rental properties offer a unique combination of income generation and potential for appreciation. Here's what makes them attractive:

- **Passive Income:** Rental properties provide a steady stream of income through monthly rent payments. This income can contribute significantly to your financial goals and overall wealth creation.
- **Appreciation Potential:** Over time, the value of your property may increase due to market trends or improvements you make. This appreciation can be a significant source of wealth when you eventually sell the property.
- **Tax Advantages:** Rental properties offer certain tax benefits, such as deductions for depreciation, mortgage interest, and repairs. Consulting a tax advisor can help you understand the specific tax implications in your area.

However, rental properties are not a "get rich quick" scheme. They require significant upfront investment, ongoing management responsibilities, and a clear understanding of the market.

Considering Your Options: Types of Rental Properties

Before diving in, explore the various types of rental properties available:

- **Single-Family Homes:** These offer potentially higher rental income but require more upkeep and may have a smaller pool of potential tenants.
- **Multi-Unit Properties:** Duplexes, triplexes, or apartment buildings offer economies of scale in terms of maintenance and management but can be more complex to manage and require stricter regulations.
- **Commercial Properties:** Investing in office spaces, retail storefronts, or industrial buildings can offer higher rental income but comes with a different set of considerations and may require specialized knowledge.

The ideal property type depends on your budget, risk tolerance, and desired level of involvement in management.

The Responsibilities of a Landlord: Beyond Rent Collection

Being a landlord comes with a responsibility to your tenants and the property itself. Here's what to expect:

- **Finding and Screening Tenants:** Thorough tenant screening is crucial to minimize risks of late payments, property damage, and eviction.
- **Maintenance and Repairs:** Rental properties require ongoing maintenance and repairs to ensure the property remains habitable and retains its value.

- **Legal Compliance:** Landlords are bound by fair housing laws and local regulations regarding tenant rights and property maintenance.
- **Vacancy Periods:** Be prepared for potential periods when your rental unit is unoccupied, resulting in loss of income.

Owning rental properties can be a rewarding experience, but it's not a passive investment. Consider hiring a property management company if you lack the time or expertise to handle these responsibilities yourself.

Financial Considerations: Calculating the Numbers

Before investing in a rental property, conduct thorough financial analysis. Factors to consider:

- **Down Payment:** Most rental properties require a significant down payment, which can be a barrier for some investors.
- **Ongoing Costs:** Factor in mortgage payments, property taxes, insurance, maintenance, and potential repairs when calculating your potential return on investment (ROI).
- **Rental Income:** Research average rental rates in your target area to estimate your potential income stream.
- **Cash Flow:** Ensure the rental income exceeds your monthly expenses to achieve positive cash flow, which contributes to your overall profitability.

Consulting with a financial advisor can be beneficial to assess your financial situation and determine if rental properties are a suitable investment for you.

The Road to Success: Strategies for Savvy Landlords

Here are some strategies to maximize your success as a landlord:

- **Location, Location, Location:** Invest in a property in a desirable location with high rental demand and potential for appreciation.
- **Be a Selective Landlord:** Meticulous tenant screening minimizes risks and ensures a smoother rental experience.
- **Maintain Your Property:** Regular maintenance keeps your property in good condition, attracts quality tenants, and retains its value.
- **Build Relationships with Contractors:** Having reliable contractors on call ensures timely and cost-effective repairs when needed.
- **Stay Up to Date with Regulations:** Familiarize yourself with evolving laws and regulations governing landlord-tenant relationships.

By employing these strategies, you'll increase your chances of success in the world of rental properties.

Rental Properties: Not for Everyone

Rental properties offer a compelling path to wealth creation but come with inherent challenges. Here's a final note of caution:

- **Real Estate Market Fluctuations:** The real estate market can experience ups and downs, potentially impacting rental income and property values.
- **Management Demands:** Rental properties require

Monthly Rentals vs. Short Term Rentals

For Renters: Monthly Rentals
Pros:
- **Stability:** You lock in a set rent price for the lease

term.
- **Security of Tenure:** Eviction is more difficult for landlords during the lease.
- **Potentially Lower Costs:** Monthly rents can be lower than the total cost of a comparable Airbnb for a month, especially in non-peak seasons.
- **Landlord Responsible for Maintenance:** The landlord typically handles repairs and upkeep.

Cons:
- **Less Flexibility:** You're locked into the lease agreement for a set period.
- **Finding the Right Fit:** Finding a unit that meets your needs can take time.
- **Limited Amenities:** You might not get the same amenities as some Airbnbs offer (e.g., stocked kitchen, unique spaces).

For Renters: Short Term Rentals
Pros:
- **Flexibility:** You can rent for shorter durations or find last-minute stays.
- **Unique Spaces:** You can find interesting and non-traditional living spaces.
- **Potential for Amenities:** Some short-term rentals (Airbnbs, VRBOs) offer amenities like hot tubs, pools, or workspaces.

Cons:
- **Potentially Higher Costs:** The total cost for a month can be higher than a traditional rental.
- **Variable Pricing:** Prices can fluctuate depending on demand.
- **Less Stability:** Your host could cancel your reservation close to your stay.
- **Uncertainties about Upkeep:** You might be responsible for minor maintenance or cleaning.

For Landlords: Monthly Rentals
Pros:
- **Steady Income:** You receive a predictable rental

income each month.
- **Less Management:** You only need to find a tenant once per lease term.
- **Lower Upfront Costs:** You don't need to furnish the property or provide amenities.

Cons:
- **Lower Potential Income:** Monthly rents might be lower than what you could earn with short-term rentals.
- **Dealing with Long-Term Issues:** Evicting a problematic tenant can be time-consuming and expensive.
- **Vacancy Periods:** You might have periods where the unit sits empty.

For Landlords: Short Term Rentals
Pros:
- **Higher Potential Income:** You can potentially earn more than traditional rentals, especially in peak seasons.
- **More Control Over Schedule:** You can block out dates for personal use.
- **Faster Turnover:** Vacancy periods are usually shorter.

Cons:
- **More Management:** You need to constantly manage bookings, cleaning, and guest communication.
- **Higher Upfront Costs:** You might need to furnish the property and provide amenities.
- **Dealing with Transient Guests:** There's a higher chance of property damage or turnover issues.
- **Local Regulations:** Some areas have restrictions on short-term rentals.

Ultimately, the best choice depends on your individual priorities and circumstances. Consider your needs for stability, flexibility, cost, and management when making your decision.

Anchor Point

This chapter discusses rental properties as an investment. It compares them to traditional housing, highlighting the potential benefits like income and appreciation, but also the management responsibilities and financial considerations involved. Ultimately, it helps you decide if rental properties are a good fit for your wealth-building goals.

Chapter 14: Earning Without the Hustle: Understanding Dividends and Interest

Imagine a scenario where your money works for you, even while you sleep. That's the magic of dividends and interest! This chapter dives into these two fundamental concepts that can significantly boost your financial well-being.

Interest: The Reward for Lending

Think of interest as a fee you earn for lending your money to someone else. Here's how it works:

- **You Deposit Money:** When you deposit money in a savings account, certificate of deposit (CD), or certain bonds, you're essentially lending your money to a bank or institution.
- **They Pay You Interest:** In exchange for using your money, the bank or institution pays you interest. This interest is a percentage of the amount you deposit, calculated over a specific period (e.g., annually, monthly).

The interest rate offered varies depending on the type of account, the length of time your money is deposited (term), and the overall financial climate. Generally, higher-risk investments offer higher potential interest rates, while lower-risk options come with lower interest rates.

Examples of Interest-Bearing Accounts:

- **Savings Accounts:** These offer easy access to your money and a low but guaranteed interest rate. This is ideal for emergency funds or short-term savings goals. Recent offerings from financial institutions with interest rates over 4.5% in the U.S is promising.

- **Certificates of Deposit (CDs):** CDs lock your money in for a predetermined period (term) in exchange for a typically higher interest rate than a savings account. Early withdrawal penalties apply if you need the money before the term ends.
- **Bonds:** These are essentially loans you make to governments or corporations. Bonds pay interest at regular intervals and return your principal amount (the original amount you invested) when the bond matures.

Dividends: A Share of the Profits

Dividends are a portion of a company's profits that are distributed to its shareholders (owners). Here's how it works:

- **You Buy Company Stock:** When you invest in a company's stock, you become a partial owner of that company.
- **They Share Profits (Sometimes):** Publicly traded companies may choose to distribute a portion of their profits to shareholders in the form of dividends. Dividends are typically paid quarterly or annually.

Important Note: Companies are not obligated to pay dividends. The decision to pay dividends and the amount distributed depend on the company's financial health, future plans, and board of directors' discretion.

Benefits of Dividends and Interest:

- **Passive Income:** Dividends and interest provide a steady stream of income without requiring active work on your part. This can be a valuable source of additional income to supplement your salary or contribute to your financial goals.
- **Compounding Growth:** If you reinvest your dividends and

interest (instead of spending them), you can benefit from compounding growth. This means your earnings generate additional earnings over time, accelerating your wealth accumulation.
- **Hedge Against Inflation:** While not always guaranteed, some investments offering interest or dividends can help hedge against inflation, which is the rising cost of goods and services. The income you receive can help maintain your purchasing power over time.

Understanding the Risks:

- **Market Fluctuations:** The value of stocks that pay dividends and the interest rates offered on savings accounts and bonds can fluctuate based on market conditions. There's always a risk that the value of your investment might decrease.
- **Company Performance:** Dividend payments depend on a company's profitability. If a company experiences financial difficulties, dividend payments might be reduced or eliminated altogether.
- **Interest Rate Risk:** As interest rates rise, the value of existing bonds (especially long-term bonds) can decrease. Conversely, when interest rates fall, existing bond values tend to rise.

Investing for Dividends and Interest:

- **Research is Key:** Before investing in dividend-paying stocks or interest-bearing accounts, thoroughly research the company or institution. Understand their financial health, track record of dividend payments, and interest rates offered.
- **Diversification is Crucial:** Don't put all your eggs in one basket. Diversify your portfolio across different asset classes (stocks, bonds, etc.) and within each class

(different company stocks or various types of bonds) to mitigate risk.
- **Consider Your Goals:** Align your investment strategy with your financial goals and risk tolerance. Dividends and interest can be suitable for long-term goals but might not be the best option for short-term needs.

By understanding the mechanics of dividends and interest, their benefits and risks, you can leverage them as powerful tools to grow your wealth and achieve your financial goals. The next chapters will delve deeper into various investment options and strategies to build a well-rounded portfolio and navigate your path to financial freedom.

Anchor Point

The chapter highlights how dividends and interest allow you to earn passively, even while you sleep. The rest of the chapter then explores the mechanisms of dividends and interest, their benefits and risks, all in the context of achieving this goal.

Chapter 15: Owning Your Destiny: Stepping into the World of Business Ownership

The dream of being your own boss, calling the shots, and building something from the ground up – that's the allure of business ownership. But before you dive headfirst into this exciting yet challenging venture, let's explore the realities of what it means to be a business owner. This chapter will equip you with the foundational knowledge to make informed decisions about embarking on your entrepreneurial journey.

The Thrill of the Ride: The Advantages of Business Ownership

Being your own boss comes with a unique set of advantages:

- **Be Your Own Captain:** You have the freedom to set your own course, make strategic decisions, and chart the future of your business based on your vision and values.
- **Reap the Rewards:** The success of your business translates directly to your financial success. Your hard work, innovation, and strategic decisions directly impact your bottom line.
- **Shape Your Industry:** You have the power to innovate, disrupt the status quo, and potentially leave your mark on your industry.
- **Building Something Special:** The journey of building a business can be incredibly rewarding. Witnessing your creation come to life and grow can be a source of immense pride and satisfaction.

However, the road to entrepreneurial success isn't paved with gold. There are significant challenges to consider.

The Grit Behind the Glory: The Challenges of Business Ownership

Business ownership demands a unique blend of skills and resilience:

- **Wearing Multiple Hats:** From marketing and sales to finance and operations, you might find yourself tackling a variety of tasks, especially in the initial stages.
- **Financial Risk and Responsibility:** The financial success of the business rests on your shoulders. Be prepared to invest your own capital, manage cash flow carefully, and navigate potential financial setbacks.
- **Long Hours and Unsteady Income:** Building a successful business often requires long hours and unwavering dedication. Your income might not be steady, particularly in the early stages of your venture.
- **The Rollercoaster of Emotions:** The entrepreneurial journey is full of ups and downs. Be prepared to face challenges, overcome obstacles, and bounce back from setbacks with unwavering determination.

Owning a business is a 24/7/365-day job. It requires a strong work ethic, a passion for your ideas, and the ability to navigate complexities and uncertainties.

Choosing Your Path: Types of Business Ownership

The business ownership landscape offers various structures, each with its own set of advantages and considerations:

- **Sole Proprietorship:** This is the simplest structure, where you are the sole owner and operator of the business. You have complete control but also unlimited liability, meaning your personal assets are on the line for business debts.
- **Partnership:** You share ownership and responsibility with

trusted members. This can provide access to skills, capital, and shared workload, but potential conflicts need to be carefully addressed through a strong partnership agreement.
- **Limited Liability Company (LLC):** This structure offers limited liability protection for the owners' personal assets. It's a popular choice for small and medium-sized businesses, offering a balance between flexibility and protection.
- **Corporation:** This is the most complex structure, often suited for larger businesses. It offers limited liability and the ability to raise capital by selling shares (stock) to investors.

The best structure for your business depends on factors like size, liability exposure, and growth goals. Consulting with a legal and financial professional can help you make the most suitable choice.

The Entrepreneurial Mindset: Essential Traits for Success

Beyond the legalities and structures, a successful entrepreneur possesses a unique mindset:

- **Passion and Perseverance:** A burning passion for your idea and the unwavering determination to see it through challenges are crucial.
- **Problem-Solving Skills:** The ability to identify and solve problems creatively and efficiently will be your constant companion.
- **Adaptability and Learning:** The business landscape is

constantly evolving. Embrace lifelong learning and be adaptable to changing market dynamics.
- **Financial Acumen:** Understanding basic financial concepts, budgeting, and managing cash flow are essential for business success.
- **Leadership Skills:** Whether leading a team or inspiring clients, strong leadership skills will be valuable assets.

By fostering these essential traits, you'll equip yourself to navigate the exciting yet demanding world of business ownership.

The following chapters will delve deeper into crucial aspects like crafting a business plan, securing funding, marketing your venture, and the legalities involved in starting and running a business. This comprehensive guide will empower you to make informed decisions and increase your chances of success on your entrepreneurial journey.

Anchor Point

The anchor point of this chapter is the decision of whether to embark on a journey of business ownership. The chapter is structured around this central question, first outlining the allure of being your own boss (The Thrill of the Ride) and then presenting the challenges to consider (The Grit Behind the Glory). By laying out both the advantages and disadvantages, the chapter aims to help you decide if business ownership is the right path for you.

Part 6: Maintaining and Protecting Your Wealth

Chapter 16: Tax Planning: Shielding Your Wealth and Maximizing Growth

Building wealth is a marathon, not a sprint. While accumulating assets and generating income are crucial, it's equally important to safeguard your hard-earned money from the ever-present bite of taxes. This chapter explores the art of tax planning, a powerful tool for protecting your wealth and maximizing its growth over time.

The Power of Tax Planning: More Money in Your Pocket

Taxes are a reality of life, but with strategic planning, you can minimize your tax burden and keep more of your hard-earned money. Here's how tax planning benefits you:

- **Increased Take-Home Pay:** By understanding tax deductions and credits, you can legally reduce your taxable income, resulting in higher take-home pay and more money to invest or save towards your financial goals.
- **Long-Term Growth:** Reduced tax liabilities free up more resources for investments. Over time, the power of compound interest can significantly amplify your wealth accumulation.
- **Peace of Mind:** Knowing you've minimized your tax obligations reduces stress and uncertainty. You can focus on building wealth with confidence.

Tax planning is not about loopholes or evading taxes; it's about leveraging the tax code to your advantage within legal boundaries.

Understanding Your Tax Landscape: Taxes 101

Before diving into strategies, let's establish a basic understanding of taxes:

- **Tax Brackets:** The income tax system uses progressive tax brackets. As your income increases, you pay a higher marginal tax rate on additional income earned.
- **Taxable Income:** This is your gross income minus deductions and exemptions allowed by law. Tax is calculated on this taxable income.
- **Deductions:** These are expenses you can subtract from your gross income to reduce your taxable income. Examples include mortgage interest, charitable contributions, and certain business expenses.
- **Tax Credits:** These are tax dollar-for-dollar reductions of your tax liability. Tax credits can be particularly beneficial for specific activities or financial situations.

Understanding these concepts lays the foundation for effective tax planning.

Strategies for Tax-Savvy Investors: Building Your Arsenal

Here are some key tax-planning strategies you can explore (consult a tax professional for personalized advice):

- **Tax-Advantaged Accounts:** Utilizing accounts like IRAs (Individual Retirement Accounts) and 401(k)s allows your contributions and, in some cases, earnings to grow tax-deferred or tax-free until withdrawal.
- **Maximize Deductions:** Identify all eligible deductions for your specific situation. This could include mortgage interest, property taxes, charitable contributions, and certain business expenses.

- **Capital Gains Strategies:** Understand how capital gains taxes are applied to investment profits. Strategies like tax-loss harvesting can help offset capital gains and minimize tax liability.
- **Retirement Planning:** Contributing to retirement accounts not only helps build your retirement nest egg but also reduces your current taxable income.
- **Record-Keeping Meticulously:** Maintain clear and organized records of your income, expenses, deductions, and investments. There are software tools available to simplify this process. But it is important to know what the tool does.

By employing these strategies, you'll be well on your way to minimizing your tax burden and maximizing your wealth growth potential.

Beyond the Basics: Seeking Professional Guidance

Tax regulations can be complex, and the best approach for your unique situation may not be readily apparent. Consider these options:

- **Tax Software:** Tax preparation software can be helpful for straightforward situations. These programs guide you through the filing process and help calculate deductions and credits.
- **Tax Accountant or Financial Advisor:** For more complex situations, consulting with a qualified tax professional can be invaluable. They can provide personalized advice based on your income, investments, and financial goals.

Investing in qualified professional guidance can save you significant amounts in taxes over the long run, making it a worthwhile expense.

Tax Planning: A Continuous Journey

Tax laws and regulations are subject to change. Make tax planning an ongoing process. Review your situation regularly, stay updated on any changes to tax laws, and adjust your strategy accordingly.

By integrating tax planning into your overall financial strategy, you'll effectively shield your wealth from unnecessary taxation and empower yourself to achieve your long-term financial goals with greater confidence. The following chapters will delve into specific investment options, wealth-building strategies, and navigating the exciting world of investing.

Anchor Point

The anchor point of this chapter is tax planning and its role in maximizing wealth growth over time. The chapter establishes the importance of minimizing tax burden for:
- Increased take-home pay
- Long-term growth through compound interest
- Peace of mind

Everything else in the chapter revolves around this central concept, explaining tax basics, strategies for tax-savvy investors, and the importance of seeking professional guidance.

Chapter 17: Risk Management: Building a Fortress for Your Wealth

Wealth creation is an exciting journey, but it's not without its challenges. Unexpected events, market fluctuations, and unforeseen circumstances can threaten your financial well-being. This chapter introduces the concept of risk management, a crucial strategy for protecting your wealth and safeguarding your financial future.

The Ever-Present Threat: Understanding Financial Risks

Financial risks are events or circumstances that could potentially lead to financial loss. Here are some common types of risks to consider:

- **Market Risk:** The value of your investments can fluctuate due to market movements. Stock prices can decline, bonds can lose value due to rising interest rates, and real estate markets can experience downturns.
- **Economic Risk:** Broad economic factors like recessions, inflation, and interest rate changes can negatively impact your investments and overall financial stability.
- **Personal Risk:** Unexpected events like job loss, illness, or disability can disrupt your income stream and derail your financial goals.
- **Liability Risk:** Accidents, lawsuits, or unforeseen liabilities can lead to significant financial losses.

By understanding the different types of risks you might face, you can develop a proactive approach to mitigating them.

The Shield and the Sword: The Tools of Risk

Management

Risk management is a proactive approach to safeguarding your wealth from potential threats. Here are some key tools you can use:

- **Diversification:** Spreading your investments across various asset classes (stocks, bonds, ETF, mutual funds, real estate, etc.) is a cornerstone of risk management. This will reduce the risk when the sector fails. If one asset class suffers losses, others might compensate, minimizing the overall impact on your portfolio. For instance, the retail industry does well between Thanksgiving and new year, and hospitality and cruise industry does well during summertime.
- **Emergency Fund:** Building a robust emergency fund helps you weather unexpected financial emergencies like job loss or medical bills. Aim to save 3-6 months of living expenses to cover unforeseen circumstances without jeopardizing your long-term financial goals. Always ensure the accessible cash is sitting in interest earning accounts.
- **Insurance:** Various insurance policies can protect you from specific risks. Life insurance safeguards your loved ones financially in case of your death. Disability insurance provides income if you're unable to work due to illness or injury. Property and liability insurance protects your assets in case of damage or unforeseen events.
- **Asset Allocation:** This refers to the distribution of your investments across different asset classes. A young investor with a long-time horizon might allocate a higher percentage to stocks for growth potential, while a retiree nearing their golden years might prioritize bonds for income and stability. Regularly rebalance your portfolio to maintain your desired asset allocation as your risk tolerance and goals evolve.
- **Financial Planning:** Working with a financial advisor can help you create a comprehensive financial plan that considers your risk tolerance, financial goals, and

investment options. A well-crafted plan will factor in risk management strategies to protect your wealth.

By employing these tools, you can build a robust financial fortress that shields your wealth from potential threats.

Risk Management: A Continuous Process

The financial landscape is dynamic, and your risk tolerance may evolve over time. Here's why risk management is an ongoing process:

- **Review Your Risk Tolerance:** As your age, financial situation, and life goals change, your risk tolerance might evolve. Regularly assess your risk tolerance and adjust your investment strategy and risk management tactics accordingly.
- **Monitor Your Portfolio:** Stay informed about market conditions and economic trends. Track your portfolio performance and make adjustments as needed to maintain your desired asset allocation and risk profile.
- **Life Changes and Adjustments:** Major life events like marriage, starting a family, or nearing retirement might necessitate adjustments to your risk management strategies. Stay proactive and adapt your financial plan to ensure your wealth remains protected throughout your life journey.

By continuously monitoring your financial situation, adapting your risk management strategy, and making informed decisions, you'll be well-equipped to navigate the ever-changing financial landscape and safeguard your wealth for the long term.

The following chapters will delve deeper into specific investment options, wealth-building strategies, and navigating the exciting world of investing. With a solid understanding of risk management, you'll be empowered to make informed decisions and build a secure financial future.

Anchor Point

The concept of risk management and its importance in protecting your wealth is the anchor point. The chapter talks about different financial risks you might face and then introduces various tools and strategies to mitigate those risks. Everything else in the chapter revolves around this central concept, explaining how to build a financial fortress against potential threats.

Chapter 18: Estate Planning: Safeguarding Your Legacy and Protecting Your Wealth

Building wealth is a commendable achievement, but true financial security extends beyond your lifetime. Estate planning ensures your assets are distributed according to your wishes after you pass away, minimizing confusion and conflict for your loved ones. This chapter explores the importance of estate planning and the tools available to create a comprehensive plan that protects your wealth and legacy.

Beyond Accumulation: Why Estate Planning Matters

Estate planning goes beyond simply writing a will. It's a holistic approach to safeguarding your assets and ensuring your wishes are carried out after you're gone. Here are some reasons why estate planning is important:

- **Protecting Your Heirs:** A well-defined estate plan minimizes confusion and potential disputes among your beneficiaries by clearly outlining how you want your assets distributed.
- **Minimizing Taxes:** Estate planning strategies can help reduce your estate's tax burden, ensuring a larger portion of your wealth reaches your intended beneficiaries.
- **Ensuring Your Wishes are Met:** Estate planning allows you to make informed decisions about how your assets are distributed, charitable contributions are made, and even how you wish your care to be handled in case of incapacity.
- **Providing for Dependents:** If you have young children or dependents, estate planning allows you to designate guardians and ensure their financial security in your

absence.

By neglecting estate planning, you risk leaving your loved ones navigating a complex legal process during a difficult time.

The Pillars of Estate Planning: Essential Documents and Strategies

Key components of a comprehensive estate plan:

- **Will:** This legal document outlines your wishes regarding the distribution of your assets after your death. It names an executor to handle the legal aspects of settling your estate and beneficiaries who will inherit your assets.
- **Trusts:** Trusts can be valuable tools for managing and distributing assets. There are different types of trusts serving a specific purpose. A revocable living trust, for example, allows you to retain control of assets during your lifetime while ensuring they are distributed according to your wishes after your passing.
- **Power of Attorney:** This document allows you to designate someone you trust to make financial and legal decisions on your behalf if you become incapacitated.
- **Beneficiary Designations:** Review your retirement accounts, life insurance policies, and other investment vehicles to ensure beneficiaries are accurately designated. This ensures these assets pass directly to your intended recipients without going through probate, a lengthy legal process.

Consulting with an estate planning attorney is crucial to determine the most suitable strategies for your unique situation.

Planning for Incapacity: Beyond Asset

Distribution

Estate planning encompasses both after your death as well as planning for situations where you might be incapacitated and unable to make decisions for yourself:

- **Living Will (Advance Directive):** This document specifies your wishes regarding medical treatment in case you are unable to communicate them yourself.
- **Durable Power of Attorney for Healthcare:** This document allows you to designate someone you trust to make medical decisions on your behalf if you cannot do so yourself.

These documents ensure your wishes are respected and your healthcare needs are met in case of unforeseen circumstances.

Open Communication: The Heart of Effective Estate Planning

Effective estate planning extends beyond legal documents. Be open with your communication with loved ones:

- **Discuss Your Wishes:** Talk to your family members and beneficiaries about your estate plan and your wishes for your assets. Transparency fosters understanding and minimizes potential conflicts.
- **Review Regularly:** Your estate plan should be reviewed and updated periodically to reflect changes in your life, such as marriage, birth of children, or changes in your financial situation.

Open communication and ongoing review ensure your estate plan remains relevant and reflects your evolving wishes.

Estate Planning: Peace of Mind for You and Your Loved Ones

Estate planning isn't just about safeguarding your wealth; it's about providing peace of mind for yourself and your loved ones. By taking the time to create a comprehensive plan, you ensure your legacy is honored, your assets are distributed according to your wishes, and your loved ones are taken care of during a difficult time.

The following chapters will delve deeper into specific investment options, wealth-building strategies, and navigating the exciting world of investing. With a solid foundation in estate planning, you can focus on building wealth with confidence, knowing your legacy is secure.

Anchor Point

The anchor point of this chapter is the importance of estate planning. It argues that estate planning goes beyond simply accumulating wealth and ensures your wishes are carried out after you pass away, minimizing burdens on your loved ones.

Part 7: The Psychological Journey to Financial Freedom

Chapter 19: Mindset Shifts: Reprogramming Your Beliefs for Financial Freedom

The road to financial freedom starts not in your bank account, but in your mind. Our financial behaviors are deeply rooted in our beliefs and attitudes towards money. This chapter explores the crucial concept of mindset shifts – transforming your thinking patterns to empower you on your journey towards financial freedom.

The Beliefs That Bind Us: Identifying Limiting Beliefs

We all carry financial baggage – limiting beliefs inherited from family, societal norms, or past experiences. They can hold us back from achieving financial success. Here are some common limiting beliefs to be aware of:

- **Scarcity Mentality:** The belief that money is a finite resource, leading to feelings of fear and holding back from taking financial risks.
- **Instant Gratification:** Prioritizing immediate pleasure over long-term financial goals, leading to impulse spending and hindering wealth accumulation.
- **Debt Aversion:** An extreme fear of debt, preventing you from utilizing good debt (like mortgages) to build assets and achieve financial goals.
- **Victim Mentality:** Blaming external factors for your financial situation, relinquishing control and hindering proactive financial planning.
- **Not Smart Enough:** You might doubt your ability to manage money or make sound financial decisions.
- **Get Rich Quick Schemes**: Believing only unrealistic shortcuts lead to wealth can make you miss out on solid strategies.

- **Fear of Failure:** The fear of losing money can paralyze you from taking calculated risks that could lead to growth.

Identifying your limiting beliefs is the first step towards overcoming them.

Reprogramming for Success: Cultivating Empowering Beliefs

Financial freedom requires replacing limiting beliefs with empowering ones. Here are some positive mindsets to cultivate:

- **Abundance Mentality:** Believing there is enough wealth and opportunity for everyone, fostering a sense of security and encouraging goal pursuit.
- **Delayed Gratification:** The ability to prioritize long-term financial goals over fleeting desires, leading to responsible spending and saving habits.
- **Good Debt vs. Bad Debt:** Understanding that not all debt is created equal. Strategic use of good debt (like mortgages) can be a powerful tool for building wealth.
- **Empowerment Mentality:** Taking responsibility for your financial situation and believing in your ability to achieve your goals through planning, effort, and smart financial decisions.

By consciously replacing limiting beliefs with empowering ones, you shift your mindset from scarcity to abundance, fear to confidence, and from a passive to an active role in shaping your financial future.

The Power of Visualization: Seeing Your Financial Future Clearly

Visualization is a powerful tool for rewiring your brain for financial success. Here's how it works:

- **Imagine Your Goals:** Spend time vividly visualizing your financial goals. See yourself achieving your desired lifestyle, feeling secure, and in control of your finances.
- **Feel the Emotions:** Don't just see your goals; feel the emotions associated with achieving them. Feel the sense of security, freedom, and satisfaction that comes with financial freedom.

- **Bridge the Gap:** Once you've visualized your goals and the associated emotions, identify the steps you need to take to bridge the gap between your current reality and your desired future.

Visualization is not a magic bullet, but it's a powerful tool that can reprogram your subconscious mind, increase motivation, and propel you towards your financial dreams.

Building Positive Habits: From Intention to Action

Mindset shifts are essential, but they need to be translated into concrete actions. Here's how to develop positive financial habits:

- **Track Your Spending:** Awareness is the first step towards change. Track your income and expenses down to the penny.
- **Budgeting for Success:** Create a realistic budget that allocates your income towards your needs, savings goals, and responsible spending.
- **Automate Your Finances:** Set up automatic transfers to savings and investment accounts, making saving a seamless part of your financial routine.
- **Celebrate Milestones:** Acknowledge and celebrate your progress, no matter how small. This reinforces positive financial behaviors and keeps you motivated.

By consistently practicing positive financial habits, you solidify the mindset shifts you've cultivated, turning your financial goals from aspirations to achievable realities.

The Mindset Journey: A Lifelong Commitment

Financial freedom is not a destination; it's a journey. Here's why a lifelong commitment to mindset shifts is crucial:

- **External Influences:** Societal messages, advertising, and peer pressure can constantly challenge your financial mindset. Stay vigilant and reaffirm your empowering beliefs.
- **Life Changes:** Unexpected life events can test your financial resolve. Adapt your strategies while staying true to your long-term goals.
- **Continuous Learning:** Embrace lifelong learning to stay informed and adapt your strategies as needed. The financial landscape is constantly evolving. Example, recent global interest in crypto currencies.

By continuously monitoring your mindset, reinforcing empowering beliefs, and adapting to changing circumstances, you'll ensure your financial journey remains on track towards achieving your long-term goals of financial freedom.

Anchor Point

The anchor point is the concept of **mindset shifts** and their importance in achieving financial freedom. The chapter argues that financial success starts with transforming your thinking patterns from limiting beliefs to empowering ones. It emphasizes how these mindset shifts can impact your financial behaviors and ultimately your journey towards financial freedom.

Chapter 20: Lifestyle Adjustments: Living Well Within Your Means on the Path to Freedom

The road to financial freedom isn't paved with deprivation; it's about making conscious choices and aligning your lifestyle with your financial goals. This chapter explores the concept of lifestyle adjustments – smart tweaks to your everyday habits that free up resources and empower you to save and invest more. Don't worry, it's not about sacrificing all enjoyment; it's about finding creative ways to live well within your means.

Reframing Your Perspective: From Frugality to Financial Freedom

Many people associate financial freedom with extreme frugality and deprivation. However, a sustainable approach focuses on value and intentionality. Here's the shift in perspective:

- **Frugal vs. Intentional:** Frugality often implies sacrifice and deprivation. Intentionality, on the other hand, emphasizes making conscious choices that align with your values and financial goals. You're not just saving money; you're investing in your future freedom.

By viewing lifestyle adjustments as an empowering step towards financial freedom, you'll find the process more sustainable and enjoyable.

Prioritizing Needs vs. Wants: Where to Begin

The cornerstone of intentional living is differentiating between needs and wants. Here's how to identify areas for adjustments:

- **Needs Analysis:** Start by listing your essential needs – housing, food, utilities, transportation, healthcare. These are non-negotiables that ensure your well-being.
- **Wants vs. Desires:** Differentiate between fleeting desires and genuine wants. Do you truly need that expensive coffee every day, or can you brew a delicious cup at home? Prioritize experiences and activities that enrich your life over fleeting purchases.

By clearly defining your needs and prioritizing them over wants, your free up resources to allocate towards your financial goals.

Finding Value and Avoiding Impulse Purchases

Living intentionally doesn't have to mean sacrificing quality. Here are strategies to find value and avoid impulse spending:

- **Cook More at Home:** Eating out frequently can be a significant budget drain. Explore the joys of home cooking – it's healthier, often tastier, and significantly cheaper.
- **Embrace Free Entertainment:** There are countless free or low-cost ways to have fun – explore parks, museums with free admission days, or host potlucks with friends.
- **Challenge Yourself with DIY:** Before buying something new, consider if it's a project you can tackle yourself. Learning basic repairs or DIY projects can save you money in the long run.
- **Unsubscribe from Temptations:** Unsubscribe from marketing emails and avoid browsing online stores during moments of weakness. Like I mentioned in the earlier chapter, do not browse the food court when hungry.
- **Embrace the Power of Comparison Shopping:** Before

making a purchase, compare prices online and at different stores. Consider buying gently used items or exploring second-hand stores.

By being mindful of your spending triggers and finding alternative ways to fulfill your needs and wants, you'll save money without feeling deprived.

Redefining Your Definition of Luxury

Financial freedom allows you the freedom to define luxury on your own terms. Here's how to shift your perspective:

- **Experiences over Possessions:** Prioritize experiences that create lasting memories over accumulating material possessions. Invest in travel adventures, learning new skills, or spending quality time with loved ones.
- **Quality over Quantity:** Invest in fewer, high-quality items that will last longer and bring you more joy than buying cheap, disposable products.
- **Time as a Luxury:** Financial freedom allows you to control your time. Focus on activities that bring you fulfillment and reduce commitments that drain your energy and resources.

By redefining luxury as experiences, quality, and control over your time, you'll find true fulfillment on your journey to financial freedom.

Lifestyle Adjustments: A Continuous Journey

Remember, financial freedom is a marathon, not a sprint. Here's why a long-term perspective is very important:

- **Small Changes, Big Impact:** Focus on making small,

sustainable adjustments to your lifestyle. These changes will compound over time, leading to significant financial progress.
- **Celebrate Milestones:** Acknowledge and celebrate your progress, no matter how small. Reward yourself for reaching savings goals or sticking to your budget.
- **Adapting to Life Changes:** As your life evolves, your financial priorities might change. Be flexible and adapt your lifestyle adjustments accordingly.

By viewing lifestyle adjustments as a continuous journey of optimization and intentionality, you'll empower yourself to live a fulfilling life while steadily progressing towards your financial goals and achieving true freedom.

Anchor Point

The entire chapter revolves around this concept of **financial freedom**, explaining how to achieve it through intentional lifestyle adjustments. The text contrasts financial freedom with frugality, emphasizes prioritizing needs over wants, and reframes finding value and avoiding impulse purchases as strategies on the path to financial freedom. Finally, it redefines luxury in the context of financial freedom, all with the goal of achieving this state.

Part 8: The Global Tiny House Phenomenon

Chapter 21: Downsizing the Dream: The Global Tiny House Phenomenon

The traditional McMansion may be giving way to a more modest monarch: the tiny house. This global phenomenon has captured the imaginations of people seeking a simpler, more sustainable way of life. But what exactly is the tiny house movement, and why is it taking root across the world?

Small Space, Big Dreams

Tiny houses are typically defined as dwellings under 400 square feet (37 square meters). They come in a variety of styles, from trailers converted into cozy havens to architecturally designed wonders on wheels. The movement itself is multifaceted, encompassing a desire for:

- **Financial Freedom:** Tiny houses offer a lower upfront cost and reduced utility bills compared to traditional homes. This allows homeowners to break free from mortgages and live a debt-free life.
- **Environmental Consciousness:** With a smaller footprint, tiny houses use fewer resources to build, maintain, and heat or cool. This resonates with people seeking to minimize their environmental impact.
- **Simpler Living:** By downsizing their living space, tiny house dwellers often embrace minimalism, focusing on experiences and relationships rather than material possessions.

A Global Movement Takes Root

The tiny house movement isn't confined to North America. Across the globe, people are finding ways to adapt the concept to their local contexts:

- **Community Focus:** In Europe, tiny house communities are popping up, offering residents shared amenities and a sense of belonging.
- **Disaster Relief:** In Japan, tiny houses have been used as temporary housing after natural disasters, providing quick and efficient shelter.
- **Alternative Living:** In developing countries, tiny houses offer a low-cost and sustainable housing option for those priced out of traditional housing markets.

Challenges and Considerations

Despite its allure, the tiny house movement faces hurdles. Zoning regulations, lack of infrastructure in certain areas, and social stigma can make it difficult to find a legal place to park a tiny home. Additionally, living in a tiny house isn't for everyone. It requires a certain level of adaptability and comfort with close quarters.

The Future of Tiny Living

The tiny house movement is more than just a housing trend; it's a cultural shift. As people grapple with issues of affordability, sustainability, and escaping the pressures of consumerism, the tiny house offers a compelling alternative. Whether it's a permanent dwelling or a steppingstone to a more mindful way of life, the tiny house movement is here to stay, encouraging us to re-evaluate our relationship with space, possessions, and ultimately, the way we choose to live.

Anchor Point

The anchor point of this chapter is the **tiny house movement**. The entire passage revolves around defining tiny houses, exploring the reasons behind their rising popularity, and discussing the global impact of this movement.

Chapter 22 - Deep Dive: Delving into the Tiny House Phenomenon

Earlier chapters provided a broad overview of the tiny house movement. Now, let's unpack this further:

Financial Freedom vs. Hidden Costs:

- While tiny houses boast lower upfront costs, there can be hidden expenses. Building permits, finding legal parking, and connecting to utilities can add up.
- Financing options for tiny houses are also limited compared to traditional homes.

Sustainability:

- Tiny houses can be incredibly eco-friendly, using recycled materials and promoting lower energy consumption. However, the environmental impact also depends on factors like the building materials chosen and how the tiny house is powered.

The Minimalist Mindset:

- Living in a tiny house necessitates a shift towards minimalism.
- Decluttering and prioritizing experiences over possessions are key aspects of adapting to a smaller space.

Global Adaptations:

- **Latin America:** Here, tiny houses are seen to address housing shortages and poverty.

- **Asia:** Tiny houses in Asia often incorporate traditional design elements and sustainable practices.

Social and Legal Challenges:

- Zoning regulations are a major hurdle for tiny house dwellers. Many areas don't have clear guidelines for these dwellings.
- Building codes often make it difficult to get a tiny house certified as a permanent residence.

Beyond the Tiny House:

- The tiny house movement has inspired other small living movements, like micro-apartments in urban areas.
- The concept of downsizing and focusing on experiences over possessions is influencing broader lifestyle choices.

The Future of Tiny Living:

- Technological advancements in areas like prefabricated housing and sustainable materials could make tiny houses more affordable and efficient.
- As regulations adapt and social acceptance grows, tiny house living could become a more mainstream housing option.

Considering Going Tiny?

Before taking the plunge, thorough research is crucial. Consider factors like:

- **Lifestyle:** Tiny house living requires flexibility and a willingness to downsize.
- **Location:** Research local zoning regulations and find a legal place to park your tiny house.
- **Budget:** Factor in all potential costs, including building or buying, permits, and utilities.

The tiny house movement is a thought-provoking phenomenon with far-reaching implications. Whether you choose to embrace tiny living or not, it encourages us to question our relationship with space, possessions, and the way we want to live

The United States has a patchwork approach to tiny house construction, with regulations varying greatly between states and even localities. Here's a breakdown:

States with Established Regulations (USA as of June 2024):

- **Maine:** The first state to adopt statewide building codes specifically for tiny houses.

States Generally Considered Tiny House Friendly:

- **Colorado:** Open building codes and a growing tiny housing community.
- **Texas:** Relatively relaxed regulations and many tiny house builders.
- **Oregon:** Supportive policies and a growing acceptance of alternative housing options.

- **California:** Despite a lack of statewide regulations, many areas are welcoming to tiny houses on foundations or as Accessory Dwelling Units (ADUs).

Challenges in Some States:

- **New York:** Strict building codes and zoning regulations can make tiny house living difficult.
- **Massachusetts:** Similar challenges to New York, with limited options for tiny house dwellers.
- **New Jersey:** Densely populated areas and stringent regulations can make it hard to find a place for a tiny house.

General Tips:

- **Research is Key:** Regardless of location, researching local zoning codes and building requirements is crucial before starting construction.
- **Focus on ADUs:** Investigate Accessory Dwelling Unit (ADU) regulations in your area. ADUs are small secondary dwellings on a property with a primary residence and can be a good option for tiny house living.
- **Consider Tiny House on Wheels:** If regulations are restrictive, building a tiny house on wheels (THOW) might be an option. However, finding legal parking for a THOW can be challenging.

Remember, the tiny house movement is constantly evolving, and state regulations can change. It's important to stay up to date on the latest information before embarking on your tiny house journey.

Anchor Point

The anchor point is still the **tiny house movement**, but with a focus on the practical considerations of living tiny. This chapter dives deeper into the challenges and considerations one might face when going tiny, such as financial limitations, legal restrictions, and adapting to a minimalist lifestyle. It also explores how the tiny house movement is inspiring broader trends and examines the future potential of tiny living.

Part 9: The FIRE Movement

Chapter 23: Escape the Hamster Wheel - The FIRE Movement

Imagine a world where you aren't chained to a desk job, counting down the days until retirement. The FIRE movement offers a path to just that – achieving financial independence and retiring much earlier than traditional plans. This chapter will delve into the core concepts of FIRE, its philosophy, and the strategies it employs to break free from the nine-to-five grind.

The FIRE Flame

FIRE stands for Financial Independence, Retire Early. It's a financial philosophy that emphasizes aggressive saving, investing, and mindful spending habits. Proponents of FIRE aim to accumulate enough wealth to cover their living expenses without relying on a traditional paycheck. This allows them to retire much earlier than the typical retirement age, often in their 30s or 40s.

Why FIRE?

The FIRE movement attracts individuals yearning for more control over their time and lifestyle. They might dream of pursuing passions, spending time with family, or traveling the world without being constrained by work schedules. FIRE offers the freedom to design a life on their own terms, not dictated by a job.

The FIRE Formula

Achieving FIRE hinges on two key concepts: the FIRE number and the withdrawal rate.

- **The FIRE Number:** This represents the total amount of money you'll need to cover your living expenses throughout your retirement. A common rule of thumb is the 25x rule, which suggests saving 25 times your annual expenses to achieve financial independence.
- **The Withdrawal Rate:** This refers to the percentage of your savings you can safely withdraw each year to cover your living costs in retirement. The 4% rule is a popular guideline, suggesting a withdrawal rate of 4% per year from your retirement nest egg. This withdrawal rate is believed to allow your savings to last for at least 30 years, accounting for inflation.

The FIRE Strategies

Reaching financial independence requires discipline and strategic planning. Here are some common tactics employed by FIRE followers:

- **Extreme Savings:** FIRE adherents prioritize saving a significant portion of their income, often exceeding 50%. This might involve budgeting, cutting unnecessary expenses, and living a minimalist lifestyle.
- **Boosting Income:** FIRE isn't just about spending less; it's also about earning more. Many FIRE enthusiasts explore side hustle, invest in income-generating assets, or negotiate for higher salaries.
- **Investing Wisely:** FIRE followers typically invest their savings aggressively in stocks, bonds, or real estate to grow their wealth and generate passive income.

Variations of FIRE

The FIRE movement isn't a one-size-fits-all approach. Here are some popular variations:

- **Lean FIRE:** This focuses on achieving financial independence with a lower budget and a more frugal lifestyle.
- **Fat FIRE:** This allows for a more luxurious retirement lifestyle by accumulating a larger nest egg.
- **Coast FIRE:** This involves saving enough to cover basic living expenses early in your career, then letting your investments grow to cover future expenses.

Is FIRE Right for You?

The FIRE movement offers an attractive path to early retirement and financial freedom. However, it requires dedication, discipline, and a certain level of risk tolerance. Carefully consider your lifestyle preferences, financial situation, and risk tolerance before embarking on your FIRE journey.

This chapter has provided a foundational understanding of the FIRE movement. In the following chapters, we'll delve deeper into the practical aspects of achieving financial independence, explore strategies for saving, investing, and building passive income streams. We'll also address the challenges and considerations involved in the FIRE journey, helping you decide if this path is the right fit for your unique goals and aspirations.

Anchor Point

The entire chapter revolves around explaining the core concepts of FIRE, its philosophy, and the strategies it uses to achieve early retirement. It explores the reasons why someone might choose FIRE, the calculations involved (FIRE number and withdrawal rate), and different variations within the movement itself.

Chapter 24: Beyond the Basics: A Deeper Dive into FIRE

The introductory chapter ignited the spark of the FIRE movement. Now, let's delve deeper into the practicalities and intricacies involved in achieving financial independence and early retirement.

The FIRE Number: A Customized Calculation

While the 25x rule offers a starting point, your FIRE number is highly personal. Here's how to refine it:

- **Factor in Location:** Living costs vary dramatically. Consider if you move to a lower-cost area in retirement.
- **Healthcare Expenses:** Project your future healthcare needs, especially as you age.
- **Debt Obligations:** Factor in any existing or potential debt, like student loans or mortgages, into your calculations.

Advanced FIRE Math:

For a more precise FIRE number, consider using online calculators or consulting a financial advisor. These tools can incorporate factors like inflation, taxes, and potential investment returns to provide a more personalized estimate.

The Withdrawal Rate: Nuances and Considerations

The 4% rule is a historical guideline, but it's not a foolproof guarantee. Here's what to consider when determining your withdrawal rate:

- **Market Fluctuations:** Stock market downturns can impact your nest egg. Consider a more conservative withdrawal rate (3% or below) if you're risk averse.
- **Sequence of Returns Risk:** Early retirees face a higher risk of experiencing a market downturn early in their retirement. Strategies like delaying withdrawals during downturns can help mitigate this risk.

Living on Less, But Living Well

The FIRE movement doesn't necessitate complete deprivation. Here's how to achieve a fulfilling life with mindful spending:

- **Differentiate Needs from Wants:** Clearly define your essential needs (housing, food, healthcare) and distinguish them from fleeting desires.
- **Embrace Frugal Fun:** Explore free or low-cost activities that bring you joy, like hiking, volunteering, or visiting local attractions.
- **DIY and Resourcefulness:** Learn to repair items, cook at home, and find creative ways to entertain yourself without breaking the bank.

Building Your FIRE Arsenal: Strategies for Success

FIRE isn't just about saving money; it's about strategic wealth creation. Here are some effective strategies:

- **Increase Your Income:** Negotiate a raise, explore side hustles, or pursue career advancement opportunities. Passive income streams from rental properties or royalties can also be beneficial.
- **Invest Wisely:** Diversify your portfolio across stocks, bonds, and real estate to manage risk and maximize returns. Consider low-cost index funds for a balanced

approach.
- **Automate Your Finances:** Set up automatic transfers to savings and investment accounts to ensure consistent progress towards your goals.

The FIRE Journey: Challenges and Considerations

The path to FIRE isn't always smooth sailing. There are some potential roadblocks to consider:

- **Delayed Gratification:** FIRE requires sacrificing some current desires for future freedom. Are you prepared to make those trade-offs?
- **Market Volatility:** Investment markets fluctuate. Be prepared for potential downturns and adjust your strategy accordingly.
- **Lifestyle Changes:** Early retirement might necessitate a change in your lifestyle. Ensure you're comfortable with a potentially lower income in retirement.

Is FIRE Right for You?

The FIRE movement offers an attractive path to financial independence. However, it's not a guaranteed fit for everyone. Here are some questions to ask yourself:

- **What are your priorities?** Do you value financial freedom over a high-paying career with its perks?
- **What is your risk tolerance?** Are you comfortable with market fluctuations and potential setbacks?
- **What is your ideal retirement lifestyle?** Can you envision yourself living comfortably on a potentially reduced income?

By carefully considering these factors, you can determine if the FIRE movement aligns with your values and aspirations.

Anchor Point

The entire passage revolves around achieving Financial Independence and Early Retirement (FIRE). Calculating your FIRE number is the first step outlined and serves as the foundation for all the following discussions on withdrawal rates, living expenses, and strategies to build wealth.

Chapter 25: Tailoring the Flame: Variations of the FIRE Movement

The FIRE movement isn't a monolith. It offers a spectrum of approaches to achieve financial independence and early retirement. This chapter explores some popular variations, allowing you to find the path that best suits your lifestyle and aspirations.

Lean FIRE: Freedom on a Budget

Lean FIRE prioritizes achieving financial independence with a minimalist lifestyle. Proponents aim to save a high percentage of their income (often exceeding 70%) and live frugally to reach their FIRE number faster.

- **Pros:** Earlier retirement and lower risk of running out of money in retirement.
- **Cons:** Requires significant sacrifices in terms of lifestyle and material possessions.

Fat FIRE: Early Retirement in Luxury

Fat FIRE caters to those who desire a luxurious lifestyle in retirement. This approach necessitates accumulating a larger nest egg to support a higher standard of living.

- **Pros:** Allows for greater flexibility and indulgence in retirement.
- **Cons:** Requires a longer accumulation phase and a higher tolerance for risk.

Coast FIRE: Taking a Break from the Grind

Coast FIRE focuses on saving enough to cover basic living expenses early in your career. You can then continue working, but with the knowledge that your investments will eventually support your desired lifestyle.

- **Pros:** Reduces work stress by offering a safety net and the option to work part-time or pursue passion projects later.
- **Cons:** Requires careful planning and a longer timeframe to achieve full financial independence.

Barista FIRE: Part-Time Freedom

Barista FIRE involves achieving a FIRE number that covers most living expenses, with a part-time job supplementing your income in retirement. This can provide health insurance benefits and a social outlet.

- **Pros:** Allows for early retirement with some continued income and social interaction.
- **Cons:** Requires careful budgeting and finding enjoyable part-time work in retirement.

Semi-Retirement FIRE:

This approach involves transitioning gradually from full-time work to a reduced schedule, allowing for more free time while still generating income.

- **Pros:** Provides a smooth transition to retirement and offers a sense of purpose through continued work.
- **Cons:** May require career flexibility and finding an employer who allows for a reduced workload.

Choosing Your FIRE Path

The right FIRE variation depends on your individual goals and preferences. Here are some factors to consider:

- **Desired Lifestyle:** How much do you spend, and what kind of retirement do you envision?
- **Risk Tolerance:** Are you comfortable with a lower nest egg and potentially working part-time in retirement?
- **Income Potential:** Can you significantly increase your income through career advancement or side hustles?

Beyond the Labels:

Remember, these variations are just starting points. You can create your own hybrid approach that blends elements from different FIRE philosophies. Experiment, adjust your strategy as needed, and most importantly, enjoy the journey towards financial independence.

Anchor Point

The entire chapter revolves around explaining the FIRE movement and its various approaches (Lean FIRE, Fat FIRE,

Coast FIRE etc.). It uses these variations as different paths to reach the goal of FIRE.

Chapter 26: Stoking the FIRE: Practical Strategies for Success

The FIRE movement offers an exciting path to early retirement. But how do you get there? This chapter tackles the nitty-gritty – practical strategies to supercharge your savings, invest wisely, and build passive income streams that will propel you towards financial independence.

Saving Strategies: Squeezing the Most Out of Your Income

- **Track Your Expenses:** Identify areas where you can cut back. Utilize budgeting apps or spreadsheets to monitor spending patterns.
- **Embrace Frugal Living:** Explore low-cost alternatives for entertainment, dining, and transportation. Consider home-cooked meals, free or low-cost hobbies, and utilizing public transport.
- **Debt Reduction:** High-interest debt can derail your FIRE plans. Prioritize paying off credit cards and other high-interest loans. Consider debt consolidation strategies to lower interest rates.
- **Increase Savings Rate:** Aim to save a significant portion of your income – ideally 50% or more. Consider automatic transfers to savings or retirement accounts to ensure consistent saving.
- **Negotiate Raises:** Don't undervalue your worth! Research your industry standard and negotiate for a raise to boost your income.

Investment Strategies: Growing Your Wealth for the Long Term

- **Diversify Your Portfolio:** We talked about this in an earlier chapter. Invest across different asset classes like stocks, bonds, and real estate to manage risk and

maximize returns.
- **Low-Cost Index Funds:** Consider low-cost index funds that track broad market indexes. These offer a passive investment approach with historically strong returns and minimal management fees.
- **Tax-Advantaged Accounts:** Maximize your contributions to tax-advantaged retirement accounts like IRAs and 401(k)s. These accounts offer tax benefits on contributions and potentially tax-free growth.
- **Rebalance Your Portfolio Regularly:** Periodically rebalance your portfolio to maintain your desired asset allocation. This ensures your investments stay aligned with your risk tolerance and long-term goals.
- **Educate Yourself:** Continuously learn about investing strategies and market trends. Read financial publications, listen to podcasts, or consider consulting a financial advisor for personalized guidance.

Building Passive Income Streams:

Passive income is a game-changer in the FIRE journey. Few options below:

- **Rental Properties:** Investing in rental properties can provide a steady stream of income while the property appreciates in value over time. However, it requires upfront capital and ongoing management responsibilities.
- **Peer-to-Peer Lending:** Consider online platforms that connect lenders with borrowers. Carefully evaluate borrower risk profiles and choose platforms with robust security measures.
- **Dividends:** Investing in dividend-paying stocks can provide a regular stream of income. However, dividends aren't guaranteed, and the stock price can fluctuate.
- **Side Hustles:** Develop a side hustle that aligns with

your skills and interests. This could be freelancing, online businesses, or crafting and selling products.
- **Gig Work:** Several online service providers are popping up fulfilling specific needs. E.g., Angie's List – for handyman services, UPWORK – access to global workers.

Remember:

There's no one-size-fits-all approach. Experiment with different strategies, find what works best for you, and constantly refine your approach as your income, expenses, and risk tolerance evolve.

Anchor Point

The anchor point of this chapter is **achieving financial independence and early retirement (FIRE)**.

Like the previous chapter, everything in this section focuses on providing practical steps to reach the ultimate goal of FIRE. It details strategies for saving money, investing wisely, and generating passive income streams – all geared towards financial independence.

Chapter 27: Navigating the Roadblocks: Challenges and Considerations on the FIRE Path

The FIRE journey is an exciting adventure, but it's not without its bumps and detours. This chapter explores the challenges you might encounter and offers resources to stay motivated and on track towards your goal of financial independence and early retirement.

Challenges and Considerations

- **Delayed Gratification:** The FIRE journey often requires sacrificing current desires for future freedom. Are you prepared to say no to expensive habits and prioritize saving?
- **Market Volatility:** Investment markets fluctuate, and your nest egg can be impacted by downturns. Be comfortable with a degree of risk and have a plan to weather potential storms.
- **Lifestyle Changes:** Early retirement might necessitate significant lifestyle changes. Can you envision yourself living comfortably on a potentially reduced income?
- **Unexpected Expenses:** Life throws curveballs. Factor in potential emergency funds and healthcare costs when calculating your FIRE number.
- **Social Pressures:** Society often equates success with a high-paying career. Be prepared to explain your choices and resist pressures to conform to traditional work models.

Staying Motivated and On Track

The key to FIRE success is unwavering motivation and a commitment to your long-term goals. Here are some resources and strategies to keep you fired up:

- **Build a FIRE Community:** Connect with other FIRE enthusiasts online or in local groups. Share experiences, offer support, and learn from each other's successes and challenges.
- **Visualize Your Dream Lifestyle:** Create a vision board or a detailed description of your ideal retirement. This will serve as a constant reminder of your "why" and fuel your motivation.
- **Track Your Progress:** Monitor your savings, investments, and overall progress towards your FIRE number. Celebrate milestones and use data to adjust your plan as needed.
- **Practice Gratitude:** Focus on the positive aspects of your journey. Appreciate the freedom and flexibility that come with achieving financial independence.
- **Seek Professional Guidance:** Consider consulting a financial advisor to create a personalized plan and address any financial concerns you might have.

Additional Resources

- **FIRE Blogs and Podcasts:** A wealth of information exists online. Explore blogs and podcasts dedicated to the FIRE movement. These resources can provide valuable insights, strategies, and inspiration.
- **FIRE Books:** Several books delve into the FIRE philosophy and offer practical advice on achieving financial independence. Consider reading these for in-depth knowledge and motivation.
- **Financial Calculators:** Utilize online calculators to estimate your FIRE number, investment returns, and withdrawal rates. These tools can help you refine your plans and make informed decisions.

Remember: The FIRE journey takes time to yield. Embrace the process, learn from mistakes, and celebrate the achievements. With dedication, perseverance, and the right resources, you can turn your dream of early retirement into a reality.

Anchor Point

The entire chapter talks about the challenges one might face on the vägen (Swedish for way, journey) towards FIRE and offers ways to stay motivated and on track for achieving this goal of financial independence and early retirement.

Chapter 28: The FIRE Within: A Conclusion and Call to Action

This journey through the FIRE movement has hopefully ignited a spark within you. As we conclude, let's revisit the key takeaways and empower you to take charge of your financial future.

Recap: The Pillars of FIRE

- **Financial Independence:** The core principle of FIRE is achieving a level of wealth where your investments cover your living expenses, allowing you to retire early and live life on your own terms.
- **Strategic Saving:** FIRE emphasizes aggressive saving, often exceeding 50% of your income. Budgeting, cutting unnecessary expenses, and prioritizing saving are crucial aspects.
- **Investing Wisely:** Growing your wealth through smart investments is essential. Diversification across stocks, bonds, and potentially real estate helps manage risk and maximize returns.
- **Living Frugally (or Not So Frugally):** FIRE doesn't necessitate complete deprivation. It's about mindful spending and prioritizing experiences over material possessions. Variations like Lean FIRE and Fat FIRE cater to different spending preferences.

Embrace Your FIRE Journey

The beauty of FIRE is its adaptability. There's no single path to success. Consider your lifestyle goals, risk tolerance, and financial situation to choose the FIRE variation that best aligns with your vision.

Remember:

- **Start Now:** The power of compound interest is on your side. The sooner you begin, the faster you'll reach your financial goals.
- **Growth over perfectionist mindset:** Don't be discouraged by temporary setbacks. Focus on consistent progress, even if it's a small step forward each day.
- **Enjoy the Ride:** Financial independence is a means to an end. Don't lose sight of the experiences and lifestyle you hope to achieve in early retirement.

A Final Spark of Motivation

The FIRE movement offers an opportunity to break free from the traditional mold. It's about taking control of your finances, designing a life you love, and pursuing your passions. Take what you've learned here, conduct further research, and most importantly, believe in your ability to achieve financial independence.

Light the FIRE within, and watch it illuminate your path to a future filled with freedom and possibility.

Case studies or real-life examples: Including real-life examples of people who have achieved financial freedom can make the guide more relatable and inspiring for readers.

- **Financial calculators or worksheets:** Providing financial calculators or downloadable worksheets can make it easier for readers to put the concepts into practice.
- **Glossary of financial terms:** A glossary of financial terms can be helpful for readers who are unfamiliar with some of the terminology used throughout the guide.

Anchor Point

The anchor point of this chapter is the **recap of the key takeaways** from the FIRE movement. This section serves as a foundation, reminding readers of the core principles (financial independence, strategic saving, wise investing, mindful spending) before launching into the actionable steps and motivational closing.

It essentially summarizes the crucial knowledge gained throughout the guide and grounds the reader in the essential elements of achieving financial independence through FIRE.

Part 10: Conclusion

Chapter 29: Conclusion: Reaching Your Goals, Living a Fulfilling Life

The journey to financial freedom is a marathon, not a sprint. It demands discipline, dedication, and a continuous learning mentality. This concluding chapter offers guidance on navigating your path, celebrating milestones, and ultimately living a life enriched by financial security and freedom.

Reaching Your Goals: The Roadmap to Freedom

The road to financial freedom is unique for everyone. However, some key strategies can guide your journey:

- **Maintain Your Focus:** Keep your long-term goals in mind. Visualize your desired future and use it as a source of motivation during challenging times.
- **Celebrate Milestones:** Acknowledge and celebrate your progress, no matter how small. Reaching savings goals or sticking to your budget deserves recognition. This reinforces positive financial behaviors and keeps you motivated.
- **Embrace Lifelong Learning:** The financial landscape is constantly evolving. Stay informed about investment opportunities, tax laws, and economic trends. The more you learn, the better equipped you'll be to make informed decisions and adapt your strategies.
- **Seek Professional Guidance:** Don't be afraid to seek help from qualified financial advisors or planners. They can provide personalized advice based on your unique situation and risk tolerance.
- **Be Flexible and Adaptable:** Life throws curveballs. Be prepared to adjust your strategies as your financial situation, life goals, or personal circumstances evolve.

By staying focused, celebrating your wins, and embracing continuous learning, you'll stay on track towards achieving your financial goals.

Living a Fulfilling Life: Beyond the Numbers

Financial freedom is not an end goal; it's a powerful tool to create a life you love. Here's how to leverage your financial security to live a fulfilling life:

- **Pursue Your Passions:** With financial freedom, you have the time and resources to pursue your passions, whether it's starting a business, traveling the world, or learning a new skill.
- **Give Back to Your Community:** Financial security empowers you to contribute to causes you care about. Volunteer your time or donate to charities that align with your values.
- **Spend Time with Loved Ones:** Financial freedom allows you to prioritize quality time with family and friends. Create unforgettable memories and build long term relationships.
- **Focus on Your Well-being:** Invest in your physical and mental health. Pursue healthy habits, manage stress, and prioritize activities that bring you joy and peace.

Financial freedom is not just about accumulating wealth; it's about creating a life filled with purpose, passion, and fulfillment.

The Journey Continues: Embrace the Process

The pursuit of financial freedom is an ongoing adventure. Habituate is the key:

- **Enjoy the Journey:** Focus on the positive aspects of your

financial journey – the sense of accomplishment, the growing security, and the expanding possibilities that come with achieving your goals.
- **Focus on Progress, Not Perfection:** There will be setbacks and unexpected challenges. Every step forward takes you closer to your goals.
- **Financial Freedom is a Lifelong Pursuit:** Your financial situation and goals will evolve throughout your life. Embrace the journey of continuous learning, adaptation, and growth.

Building financial freedom is a rewarding and empowering process. By following the guidance outlined in this book, committing to continuous learning, and embracing the journey, you'll be well-equipped to navigate the path to financial security and design a life filled with freedom, purpose, and fulfillment.

Anchor Point

In this final chapter, the anchor point shifts slightly compared to the previous one. While the recap served as the foundation in the earlier chapter, here the anchor point is the concept of **financial freedom as a tool for living a fulfilling life**.

The chapter starts by acknowledging the journey to financial independence and then transitions to how to leverage that freedom to create a life rich in experiences and meaning. This shift in focus from achieving financial goals to living a fulfilling life becomes the central theme that ties the various strategies and advice together.

Resources

Charlie Giattino and Esteban Ortiz-Ospina (2020) - "Are we working more than ever?" Published online at OurWorldInData.org. Retrieved from:

https://ourworldindata.org/working-more-than-ever

Cambridge English Dictionary:
https://dictionary.cambridge.org/us/dictionary/english/frugal

The Tiny House Society (https://www.tinysociety.co/) offers a state-by-state breakdown of tiny house regulations.

The American Tiny House Association (https://americantinyhouseassociation.org/) provides resources and guidance for tiny house dwellers.

Calculators
https://www.vertex42.com/Calculators/budget-calculator.html

Crypto Market https://cointelegraph.com/price-indexes

Acknowledgement

*Thanks to my wife Hema and
Our son Venkat*

www.ingramcontent.com/pod-product-compliance
Lightning Source LLC
Chambersburg PA
CBHW071925210526
45479CB00002B/564